THE BIBLE

THE BASICS

'This book introduces some of the enduring and endlessly interesting questions about the Bible and its cultural influence. The writing is clear and fluid, but never overly simplifying ... highly recommended.'

Tod Linafelt, *Georgetown University, USA*

'With characteristic lucidity and freshness, John Barton offers firm foundations for the modern student. He addresses key questions that remain relevant for the twenty-first century in a balanced and thoroughly accessible way.'

George Brooke, *University of Manchester, UK*

The Bible: The Basics is a compelling introduction to the Bible as both a sacred text, central to the faith of millions, and a classic work of Western literature, containing a tapestry of genres, voices, perspectives and images. This masterly guide skilfully addresses both aspects of the Bible's character by exploring:

- the rich variety of literary forms, from poetry to prophecy and epistles to apocalypses
- the historical, geographic and social context of the Bible
- contemporary attitudes to the Bible held by believers and non-believers
- the status of biblical interpretation today.

Including maps, a chronology and detailed suggestions for further reading, this is an ideal starting point for anyone studying the Bible in any setting or simply wanting to know more about the best-selling book of all time.

John Barton is Oriel & Laing Professor of the Interpretation of Holy Scripture at the University of Oxford. His previous books include *Reading the Old Testament*, *The Nature of Biblical Criticism* and *What is the Bible?*

The Basics

THE BIBLE

THE BASICS

John Barton

Routledge
Taylor & Francis Group

LONDON AND NEW YORK

First published 2010
by Routledge
2 Park Square, Milton Park, Abingdon, Oxon OX14 4RN

Simultaneously published in the USA and Canada
by Routledge
270 Madison Avenue, New York, NY 10016

Routledge is an imprint of the Taylor & Francis Group, an informa business

© 2010 John Barton

Typeset in Aldus by Taylor & Francis Books
Printed and bound in Great Britain by
TJ International Ltd, Padstow, Cornwall

British Library Cataloguing in Publication Data
A catalogue record for this book is available from the British Library

Library of Congress Cataloging in Publication Data
Barton, John, 1948-
The Bible – the basics / John Barton.
    p. cm.
Includes bibliographical references.
1. Bible – Introductions. I. Title.
    BS475.3.B37 2010
    220.6'1 – dc22

                    2009030702

ISBN 10: 0-415-41135-1 (hbk)
ISBN 10: 0-415-41136-X (pbk)
ISBN 10: 0-203-85998-7 (ebk)

ISBN 13: 978-0-415-41135-6 (hbk)
ISBN 13: 978-0-415-41136-3 (pbk)
ISBN 13: 978-0-203-85998-8 (ebk)

For Mary

CONTENTS

FIGURES

PREFACE

Some people love the Bible and some hate it; but few read it. Anyone who studies the Bible, whether as part of a course in theology or religious studies or for personal interest, is in a minority in the modern world. The aim of this book is to make their task easier, by providing some of the background information that can make what is now often an alien text come alive. What may happen next depends on the reader. For some a more intensive knowledge of the Bible becomes a strong support for faith, but for others it seems to reduce the text's religious claims. I have not written with any religious intention, but simply to elucidate what is often a difficult and complex book. The only underlying assumption is that the Bible is important—not a trivial or uninteresting text. It has not maintained its centrality in Western culture by sleight-of-hand, but through having things to say that still demand our attention, whatever conclusions we come to about them. But the book is emphatically *not* a work of Christian apologetics or evangelism, and I do not believe that only believers can understand the Bible properly.

In reading the book it will help to have a Bible to hand. I have quoted a good deal verbatim, but there was not space to quote every passage I wanted to refer to. My quotations are from the Revised Standard Version, which I believe is the best modern translation; but it is going out of print, and readers may therefore have to manage with the New Revised Standard Version, which

I do not think is an improvement on its predecessor, or on the New Jerusalem Bible or the Revised English Bible (these various translations are discussed in chapter 2). It does not matter very much which translation one uses, so long as one realizes that it *is* a translation—and hence that its exact wording often cannot be pressed as though it were the original.

I am very grateful to the editorial and production team at Routledge for commissioning this book and guiding it through to publication. I am also grateful to many colleagues and students for help, advice, and kindness. Above all I am grateful to my wife, Mary, to whom the book is dedicated with love.

John Barton
Oriel College, Oxford
October 2009

THE BIBLE IN THE MODERN WORLD

The Bible is central to Christianity and Judaism, but it is also a classic of Western (though originally Middle Eastern) literature. It has been read and pondered for generations, translated, paraphrased, interpreted, preached on, and dramatized. It has been praised as sublime and attacked as barbaric. Throughout the world it sells more copies than any other book. I begin this introduction to it by reflecting on how it is typically read by believers, who might be called its primary readership, before going on to explain how it is understood by academic biblical scholars.

READING THE BIBLE AS SCRIPTURE

Most people who read the Bible do so for religious reasons. The Bible is the sacred book of Christians, and the part of it that Christians call the 'Old Testament' is the sacred book of Jews. When believers read the Bible, they do not treat it as they would any other book, but approach it with expectations linked to its special sacred status. They read it 'as Scripture', and this involves a number of assumptions and attitudes that produce distinctive results. Similar effects can be seen in other religions that have sacred writings.

Most believing readers begin from the conviction that the Bible is the word of God to the Christian or Jewish community, and that the meanings to be found in it flow from this. The Scriptures, it is believed, are not simply a collection of ancient books that happen to have come together to form a corpus, but a carefully selected range of works in which there is a communication from God. For Christians this is very obviously true of the New Testament, which is the primary witness to the events of the life, death, and resurrection of Jesus of Nazareth and the beginnings of the Christian Church which he founded, including the very early testimony of the apostles, above all perhaps the Apostle Paul. But it is also true of the Old Testament, in which God is encountered throughout the history of ancient Israel, witnessed to by prophets, priests, and sages, and described by historians and psalmists. In these works, believers think, the word of life is to be found, and reading them is thus not at all the same kind of experience as reading any other books, not even other religious texts. It calls for a particular mind-set, and for a number of presuppositions about what will be found in the text. Here are five of them.

TRUTH

First, there is generally an expectation that what we find in the Bible will be *true*. For some Christians, especially on the more conservative and evangelical wings of the churches, the truth that is looked for is literal and historical truth, so that whatever the biblical text affirms is taken to be factually accurate. This is most obviously true for 'creationists'. All Jews and Christians believe that God is the creator of the world, but a creationist, in the technical sense, is one who subscribes to the literal accuracy of the first chapters of Genesis. Creationism has seen a huge upswing in recent years, especially in the USA, where there is often a demand that it be taught alongside scientific theories about the origins of the universe.

But for many who would not subscribe to this it remains the case that the Bible is to be read as true rather than as false. The truth it contains may sometimes be poetic or symbolic truth rather than factual truth. But it is not an option to suggest that anything in the Bible is an expression of error. Even if, for example, Genesis 1–2 does not accurately express the length of time it took God to create the universe, it is unacceptable to say that it is therefore simply mistaken about the events described: there is bound to be some level at which what the author wrote is true. Many Christians will say, for example, that although the idea of creation in six days is not factually accurate, the intention of showing that God is the creator remains, and this is indeed a profound truth. It would be wrong for a Christian to read Genesis 1–2 looking for fundamental error in what it is trying to tell us. Christians who are not in the least fundamentalist will usually shy away from saying that Genesis 1 is 'wrong'; generally they will say that it is profoundly true in a theological or perhaps in a poetic sense, and many are (perhaps surprisingly) quite attracted by the argument that even some of the details are much less far from scientific truth than other people think—you can often hear, for example, the argument that Genesis is really talking about six *ages* in the creation of the world and that there is some scientific evidence for this. The contention that when Genesis says 'day' it means 'day', that is, twenty-four hours, and that this is simply a mistake, does not commend itself to many Christian readers.

The same would be said about the historical books of the Bible, and for Christians perhaps especially about the Gospels. We know, from the fact that the Gospels tell significantly different versions of the story of Jesus, that they cannot all be literally true in everything they say, but this is a far cry from saying that they are false. Very often the exact detail, it is felt, doesn't matter that much, and the evangelists have captured the essence of Jesus in the way they portray him even if there are inaccuracies at the purely factual level. To take a famous example, Matthew, Mark, and Luke tell us that the 'cleansing of the Temple'—Jesus' violent ejection of traders from the temple in Jerusalem—happened towards the end of his life, and imply that it was a factor in precipitating his arrest (see Matthew 21:12–13; Mark 11:15–18; Luke 19:45–46); whereas the Gospel of John places it at the beginning of his work (see John 2:13–22). Both cannot be right at the merely historical level. But for most Christians the underlying message of the cleansing of the Temple is far more important than the 'mere' question of when exactly it happened, and that is not affected by this historical discrepancy. It is the meaning that counts, not the mere historical detail, and at that level, people feel, the story is profoundly true, whenever exactly it took place.

RELEVANCE

Second, Scripture is to be read as *relevant*. Even where, for example, Paul is discussing an issue that arose in the early Church but does not arise in the same form today (e.g. whether Christians should eat meat that has been sacrificed to false gods, as in Romans 14 or 1 Corinthians 8 and 10), this does not mean that the text in question has nothing to say to us. It is our task as readers of Scripture to discern what God is saying to us through the inclusion of such passages in the Bible. Because the Bible is authoritative, it does not have passages that were once relevant but are so no longer: all that is written is there for *our* instruction (cf. 1 Corinthians 10:11). So it is not an option, when faced with a puzzling or difficult text, to say that it simply has nothing to say to us today. The fact that it was included in the Scriptures means that it is eternally relevant to the Christian believer.

The principle of relevance seems to be built into the idea of Scripture in most, perhaps all, religions that have a sacred book. If you attend a Christian Bible-study group, it isn't an option when someone asks what the passage being studied is saying to us to reply that it isn't saying anything to us at all. The early Christians believed that everything was relevant in the very direct sense that their own life and times were actually predicted in the Scriptures of the Old Testament. Most Christians today don't see matters in this way, but they do believe that what the Bible contains is applicable in every age. To some extent of course this is true of other literature, too: many people would say that Shakespeare, for example, is perpetually relevant, and each age needs to discover him anew. But with the Bible the principle works on a more exalted plane, and means that for most Christians there is not a single sentence in Scripture that is devoid of meaning for us. In Judaism, similarly, there is a complex and sophisticated set of interpretative procedures that will guarantee the relevance of even tiny fragments of the biblical text for modern Jewish life and practice.

The contemporary relevance of the Bible can be seen very clearly in the phenomenon of Christian Zionism, a major force in the USA. Christian Zionists extract from the Bible (especially the book of Revelation and certain teachings of Jesus and Paul) a theory that the present age of the world is coming to an end quite soon. The end, in which believers will be rewarded and unbelievers punished or destroyed, must be preceded by the return of all Jews to the land of Israel, and hence Christians ought to be strongly in favour of the state of Israel and should do everything to encourage it. Only when Israel has been 'gathered in' will the end come. This explains the enthusiasm of some people in the USA for Israel—of course there are also many other reasons for supporting Israel, but this is an influential one at the moment.

PROFUNDITY

Third, everything in the Bible is *important* and *profound*. There is no triviality in Scripture, nothing that should be read as superficial or insignificant—in a way this is close to the previous point about its relevance. The Bible is a book of divine wisdom, and it does not contain any unimportant texts. This can be difficult for the average reader, who is likely to feel that some parts of Scripture are more important than others. For example, most Protestants, at least, make much more of Romans than they do of 2 John or Jude—especially since it was Romans, with its doctrine of 'justification by faith', that lay at the root of much of the Reformation. But for many believers there is strictly speaking no hierarchy within Scripture: everything is inspired by God and therefore everything is important, even if in practice we may at times concentrate more on some books than on others. We are not at liberty, for example, to regard the historical narrations in the Old Testament as mere historical records that are devoid of spiritual significance: they are all deep texts with profound meanings. That is one reason why Christians read so much of the Bible in church. Just as it isn't an option to say that something in the Bible is irrelevant to us, so it isn't an option to say that bits of it are superficial or trivial.

It is the assumed profundity of Scripture in all its parts that can lead to the practice sometimes called 'proof-texting', in which conclusions are drawn from a single verse. In secular literature we would often feel that interpretation needs to work with whole chapters, or at least with a substantial chunk of text, but in the case of the Bible it is often felt that its sanctity is found even in verses taken out of context. This may be encouraged by the practice of beginning sermons with 'a text', that is, a single verse, and deriving a great deal of teaching from it. Proof-texting may go with a belief in *verbal inspiration*, that is, the conviction that God has inspired every word of the Bible—not necessarily by literally dictating it, but certainly by ensuring that it expresses what he wants to communicate. Conservative forms of evangelicalism, especially in North and South America, and certain types of conservative Catholicism, are sometimes committed to a theory of verbal inspiration.

CONSISTENCY

Fourth, Scripture is *self-consistent*. The Christian reader must not play one part of the Bible off against another. If there appear to be contradictions between two texts, more careful reading is required so as to show that they really cohere. A classic case of this would be the apparent discord between Paul and the Letter of James over the question of 'works'. On the face of it Paul denies that human beings are made 'righteous' by good works: faith alone is needed to ensure salvation (see Galatians 3:6–14). James on the contrary affirms that good works are essential—indeed, that 'faith' apart from good works is empty and false (see James 2:18–26). There have been Christians who argued that this difference is irreconcilable, and Martin Luther famously proposed to exclude James from the Bible as worthless because it contradicts Paul. But for most Christians this is not an option. They are obliged to find ways of showing that Paul and James are not really at odds, but teach messages, which, though different in emphasis, are ultimately compatible. In a way, the self-consistency of Scripture is already implied by saying that it is true, since two messages that are incompatible with each other cannot both be true. Because Scripture thus speaks with a single voice, we can always elucidate obscure passages from more transparent ones.

The self-consistency of Scripture seems again to be a feature of many religions that have a holy text. Certainly Judaism often works with an assumption that the Bible will cohere, and there are a number of discussions in rabbinic literature designed to show that apparent discrepancies are really reconcilable; though Judaism also recognizes that texts of the Bible may sometimes be in dialogue with each other and that something positive may emerge from a kind of creative tension. In Christianity a feeling that all the holy texts must ultimately speak with the same voice lies behind 'harmonies' of the Gospels, where a coherent account is believed to underlie the apparently rather different accounts in the different Gospels. There is a long tradition of this kind of work, going back into the earliest Christian centuries. Again, Christians may sometimes think (as St Augustine of Hippo did, for example, in the fifth century) that minor discrepancies among the Gospels do not really matter since there is unanimity on the major issues of the truth of the gospel message; but most religious readers would be wary of taking this idea too far.

CONFORMITY WITH CHRISTIAN BELIEF

The first four preconditions of believing Bible-reading are shared by all Christians and in slightly different ways by Jews. The fifth is more obvious in a Catholic context, though it has parallels in the Protestant world. This is that the Bible is to be read *so as to conform to the teachings of the Church*. Catholics, for example, will normally say that where the New Testament appears to speak of Jesus' brother and sisters, the words 'brother' and 'sister' must refer to more distant relatives, because Jesus cannot have had literal brothers and sisters if, as the Church teaches, his mother remained for ever a virgin. At most they could be half-siblings from a previous marriage of Joseph's. Protestants usually do not follow this line of reasoning since they typically do not believe in the perpetual virginity of Mary, but on other matters they may well stress that the Bible is in general to be read and received within the teaching of the Church. A clear case of this would be how to read the story of the 'Fall' of Adam and Eve in Genesis 3. Christian teaching holds that Adam and Eve were created immortal but lost their immortality through the sin which brought punishment not only on them but on the whole human race. The Bible is read, especially by Protestants, as witnessing to this total depravity into which the human race has fallen, and it is not acceptable to expound it in any other way.

Like early Christian writers, religious readers typically say that the meaning passages in the Bible can have depends on consonance with the Church's teaching. If our reading implies a meaning in the biblical text that conflicts with basic Christian belief, we can be sure we have misread the text. When we read some of the Old Testament prophets, we may feel that we are hearing about a God of vindictiveness rather than of love, but that must be a mistake, since the God we worship is indeed a loving God, and we must read the prophets in the light of that belief, even if they help to highlight God's love as sometimes 'tough love'. Francis Watson puts the point I'm making here by saying that Scripture must always be interpreted with regard to 'the centre', by which he means something like what the early Christians called the 'rule of faith', a creed-like statement of what basic Christian belief is. A recent American writer expresses this by saying that Christian reading of Scripture must be 'ruled'. This belief has far-reaching consequences, since it affects what meaning one perceives any text as having: the text must always, as it were, be given the benefit of the doubt, and religious readers must never say that any text contradicts what they take to be basic Christian belief. This therefore has (as indeed do the other four principles) implications for 'exegesis'—the exposition of the meaning of the text: not just for what we 'make' of texts once we've understood them, but actually for what basic meaning we find in them in the first place.

CRITICAL READING

Alongside this kind of committed, religious reading of the Bible, there has existed from ancient times—but gathering momentum in Europe and America since the Enlightenment of the seventeenth and eighteenth centuries—an alternative approach, which is traditionally referred to as 'biblical criticism'. This is not in itself hostile to the religious authority of the Bible, but it works by 'bracketing out' religious commitment in order to read the Bible 'like any other book', in the words of the nineteenth-century scholar Benjamin Jowett. It may be that, as Jowett himself remarked, when the Bible is studied in this rather neutral way it will emerge that it is actually *un*like any other book. Shakespeare, after all, is normally read 'like any other playwright', but most people who read him in this way quickly see that he is rather special. But critical reading does not start with an assumption of specialness, but with an open and enquiring stance. It has the following features.

A LITERARY APPROACH

First, it approaches the biblical text from a *literary* rather than a religious perspective. Another way of putting this is to say that it treats the Bible as a text first, and only secondarily as in some kind of unique category (holy or inspired). It seeks to enquire into the meaning of this text in the same way that one might enquire into the meaning of any other text. (A technical way of putting this is that it does not believe in a 'special hermeneutic' for reading the Bible.) This has two important further aspects.

On the one hand, it is concerned to discover *what kind of text* each biblical book is. Reading prophecy is not the same kind of activity as reading poetry, reading historical narrative not the same kind of thing as reading law. The Gospels and the Letters of Paul belong to different literary types. One cannot legitimately treat all these different works as though they were cut from the same cloth. If we want to know how we ought to live, we shall not learn this in the same way from a Psalm or from a piece of Old Testament narrative, as from one of Paul's pieces of ethical instruction, advice given in Proverbs, or the teaching of Jesus. The various kinds of literature in the Bible cannot simply be added together to make a single work. The Bible is, as it is often put, a library of books rather than one book, and they are books of many different types, with different kinds of claim to inform the reader.

On the other hand, criticism is also concerned with the question of *when each book was written*. This is not because it regards books as limited in importance to the period they come from. Clearly, this is not the case for any major literary works—to return to Shakespeare, no one thinks that Shakespeare is important only within the Elizabethan age and has nothing to say to us. But it is vital for discovering what the text means. Words and phrases can change their meaning over time, and we need to know the historical context of expressions before we can know what they truly mean. And further, the whole meaning of an extended line of thought may make sense only once we can establish its original historical context. To return to Paul's discussion of meat sacrificed to false gods: we cannot understand this at all without some idea of the historical circumstances in which Paul lived and worked. Often (as perhaps in this case) we can work out a good deal of this from the text itself, but sometimes we need more background information. Even religious believers cannot begin to apply the text to their own situation until they know enough about its original one to see whether there really are parallels, and the general principle that 'Scripture is always relevant' is not enough to guarantee this.

NEUTRALITY

Second, critical reading, as observed already, brackets out the question of the truth of a text until it has established what the text means. Rather than believing that one can know the meaning of the text by approaching it with the correct predispositions and presuppositions, biblical critics think that the meaning emerges from reading the text 'cold', without a prior commitment to its truth or a ready-made framework (such as the Church's faith) within which it is read. Critics think of this as showing the text more *respect* than a 'committed' reading, because it does not foreclose the possibilities for what the text might turn out to mean on the basis of an already existing theory about what this meaning is bound to be. 'Bracketing out' does not mean being indifferent to the text's truth. It means seeing the question of meaning as coming first, and the question of truth second, as part of sound method. But it does have consequences which a committed religious approach might regard as undesirable. For example, it makes it impossible to know in advance whether or not two different biblical books are consistent with each other. A critical reading of Paul and James might well result in the conclusion that they really are incompatible, and that would have considerable consequences for ideas about the inspiration and authority of Scripture.

As practised over the last few hundred years, biblical criticism has resulted in some very radical conclusions about the books of the Bible. For example, it has suggested not only that some books are inconsistent with other books, but that some are even incon-sistent within themselves—in some cases to such an extent that it is hard to believe they were originally single works. 'Source criticism' has refined this discovery and argued that we can, in some cases, reconstruct the raw materials from which certain books (especially the Pentateuch—the five 'books of Moses', Genesis to

THE BIBLE IN THE MODERN WORLD   11

Deuteronomy—and the Gospels) were composed. Other types of criticism have studied the way in which different source material has been woven together to make the finished books we now have (this is generally called redaction criticism). Critical scholars have also reconstructed the history of ancient Israel and of the early Church, using the biblical text and other ancient evidence, and have sometimes produced a story strongly different from that which the Bible itself tells. In the case of the Old Testament, for example, critical scholarship has called in question the historical reality of the exodus, been doubtful about the historical existence of the 'patriarchs' (Abraham, Isaac, Jacob, and Joseph), and in recent times wondered whether anything the Bible says about even the early monarchy of Israel under David and Solomon has any claim to be historical. Even if these doubts are mistaken, biblical criticism may lead in that direction, and its findings can only be refuted by better biblical criticism, not on religious grounds.

Nowhere, perhaps, does this affect the Christian believer more than in the case of the figure of Jesus: the 'quest of the historical Jesus' has had many phases since the nineteenth century, and has resulted in pictures of Jesus very different from what emerges from an uncritical reading of the Gospels. For example, most critical scholars refuse to 'harmonize' the account in the 'Synoptic' Gospels (Matthew, Mark, and Luke—so called because they have a similar perspective) with that of John, regarding them as two strikingly variant versions of the story of Jesus. And critical reconstructions of the life of Jesus have often been greatly at variance with the Church's traditional pictures of him.

But critical study is not defined by its results, whether these are radical or conservative. What characterizes it is its approach: an open, rational approach, which treats the biblical texts like any other books from the ancient world. Many believers feel that this rational approach is at odds with a recognition of the Bible as 'special'; yet it is hard to see how someone who habitually reads books in such a critical vein can simply switch off this approach when the Bible is the book being read, and in practice biblical criticism is probably here to stay, whether one likes it or not. Can anything be said to reconcile the two approaches I have outlined and to reduce the area of conflict?

A COMPROMISE?

At the theoretical level it is hard to see how there can be any compromise between critical and 'committed' readings. They have diametrically opposed starting points. One begins with the religious community's perception of the Bible as 'Holy Scripture'; the other treats the Bible like any other book. Yet at a practical level people who practise these two approaches do in fact talk to each other. Some critical scholars come to very conservative conclusions, which are not far from those reached by religious readers even though they start from a different place. Conversely, people who read the Bible with a sense of its specialness and inspiration still have to ask about where and when its books were written, if they are not to treat it in a completely two-dimensional way. Any reader, whatever their attitude, needs to know what was the situation Paul faced in Corinth, when the prophets lived and in what sort of society they prophesied, and how the Pentateuch or the Gospels got put together. There is thus quite a lot of common ground between the two approaches I have outlined rather starkly.

The majority of critics do not deny the assumption that the Bible is important and profound: most of them would not bother to study it if they thought it trivial or insignificant. They maintain, however, that it is *possible* that given texts could, on examination, turn out to be less important than others, regarding this as an empirical question rather than as one that can be settled before reading begins. For a critic, it is only texts that could in principle turn out to be trivial that can in fact prove to be important, for otherwise importance is being attributed rather than discovered. The critical approach is always worried that more religious readers bring a meaning to the text rather than finding it there, and thus constrain the text to bear meanings that may not really be in it. But when confronted with this contrast, most people who read the text as Holy Scripture would also say that they are on a quest to understand it: they are not deliberately trying to make it mean what they already believe on other grounds.

It is also worth noting that even people with a very high view of the authority and divine inspiration of Scripture do not usually think of it as the direct utterance of God, as Muslims regard the Qur'an, but are fully aware of it as the product of human intelligence, even though that intelligence may have been guided by the spirit of God. There have been 'dictation' theories of Scripture in both Christianity and Judaism, but very few readers, however committed to the sacred character of the Bible, still embrace them. More or less everyone recognizes that the Bible had human authors, who lived therefore in particular times and places, and whose work we can to some extent come to understand. This tends to make the contrast between committed and critical readings less stark than it might seem. Thus in practice there is a large area in which Bible readers of all sorts can agree on what they find when they read Scripture. Many of both persuasions find there a message which is both important in itself and relevant in ever-new situations, and believe that they are in touch with truth.

How far is this widespread compromise really intellectually honest? Critical approaches do not simply sit alongside committed ones, but surely at some points call them in question. The discussion that follows takes the points about reading the Bible as Scripture in order.

TRUTH

First, is it the case that all parts of Scripture are true in some sense or other? We can grant that, in the case of Genesis 1, the matter being conveyed is not the detail of the six days, but the fact that God is the creator, and that this is true even if the details are not: though even here I feel sure the original author was actually intending to convey truth about historical detail, and got it wrong because he had no relevant scientific knowledge. It seems to me that he really thought the world had been created in six periods of twenty-four hours—if not, then the climax, in which God rests on the seventh day and we should do the same, no longer makes sense. But in some parts of the Bible the argument that the text is true at a theological level even if not at a historical one does not really satisfy. Are there not texts that are theologically untrue as well? For example, is the theology of the prophets, according to which the unfolding of history displays the justice of God, something we can really affirm as theologically true? Most of us nowadays do not think that the rise and fall of nations mirrors their righteousness or wickedness, as the prophets certainly believed. Furthermore, for a

Christian to assert that the self-revelation of God in Jesus surpasses what we learn of him from the 'Old Testament' seems to imply that sometimes the Old Testament did not get it right, theologically. Without rejecting the Old Testament, most Christians would certainly want to affirm that what God reveals in the New Testament surpasses it, and the earliest Christians were quite prepared to say that the Old Testament was sometimes in error— theological error, not just historical error.

RELEVANCE

Second, is it really true that everything in the Bible is relevant to our situation? Is it possible—logically possible—to produce a text that is relevant in all situations? It's tempting to say that something relevant in all situations is bound to be so general that it's really relevant in none, in any sharp sense of 'relevant'. If we are constrained by the fact that a text is Scripture to attribute to it a meaning that will have something to say to us, doesn't that mean that we are being tempted to read our own needs into it and practise what is sometimes called *eisegesis*—'reading in' to the text what we should like to find there? There must be at least a risk of this happening, and paradoxically people's very respect for the Bible can make them force it to say things they would never force a non-holy text to say. Biblical criticism stresses that in reading the text the text's own 'horizon of meaning' must come first, not our 'horizon' of need. Otherwise we are dishonouring the text we say we are treating with reverence.

PROFUNDITY

Third, is the Bible always profound? This on the whole is easier to defend. Taken out of context there are bits of the Bible that are apparently trivial—lists of names in the books of Chronicles (1 Chronicles 1, for example), or in the Gospel genealogies of Jesus (Matthew 1:1–17, Luke 3:23–38). But these texts actually contribute to larger complexes that do in nearly every case have something important and profound to say. There is not much profundity of meaning in the repeated formula in 2 Kings 'King X reigned in Jerusalem Y years, and was gathered to his fathers, and

Z his son reigned in his place'. But Kings as a whole is not a trivial or shallow book. Whether or not we can still affirm its theology, that theology is important and worth either agreeing or disagreeing with. That the Bible's profundity makes it legitimate to extract meaning from very small segments of text, however, is less obvious—that is not the way most books are read. So proof-texting is hard to reconcile with a critical reading.

CONSISTENCY

But fourth, to affirm that the Bible is wholly self-consistent seems to me a real *tour de force*. Surely Luther was right to think that James contradicts Paul, even was written in order to do so. Surely there are irreconcilable differences between the four Gospels, such that they cannot all be historically accurate; and even if historical accuracy is less important than theological accuracy, it is not totally insignificant. The Jesus of John's Gospel is not the same person as the Jesus of the other three 'Synoptic' Gospels—and indeed the picture of him is different in subtler but still important ways among the three Synoptics themselves. This may not rock the foundations of Christian faith, but it is pointless to pretend that it is not so, in the interest of 'reading the Bible as Scripture'. Some people might like to have a Bible that told a single and wholly self-consistent story, but critical study—indeed, even a careful simple reading—shows plainly that that is not the kind of Bible we have in fact got. One ought to reflect on that fact and let it have some influence on one's theories of biblical authority and inspiration, not gloss it over by claiming that there are no contradictions when it is perfectly obvious that there are.

CONFORMITY WITH CHRISTIAN BELIEF

And fifth, it is one thing to read the Bible 'in the context' of the Church's rule of faith—in the sense of letting the rule of faith guide one's own beliefs and actions, and not being too concerned when the Bible does not exactly teach what the rule says—but quite another to say that the Bible must be read as if it said exactly what the Church teaches. To return to the question of the Fall: the story in Genesis nowhere says or implies that human beings were created immortal. Indeed, it clearly implies that they were not, for once they have sinned, God ejects them from the Garden of Eden precisely to prevent the possibility that Adam may 'put forth his hand and take of the tree of life, and eat, and live forever' (Genesis 3:22). The possibility of immortality arises first at this point, and God wards it off. This must mean that the first humans were not created immortal in the first place, contrary to what St Paul teaches about death entering into the world through sin (Romans 5:12). No, they were created mortal to begin with, and death would have come their way even if they had not eaten from the tree of the knowledge of good and evil. What God threatens when he first puts them in the garden is that they will die *at once* if they eat from the tree of the knowledge of good and evil, not that they will die eventually—that is taken for granted. Furthermore, the narrative nowhere implies that they have become utterly corrupt in every possible way, only that they have disobeyed one single command. In other words, the whole edifice of Christian doctrine about the fallenness of humankind may be perfectly true, but if so this is not because it can be deduced from Genesis 3, which teaches no such thing.

Similarly, a critical reading of the New Testament makes it very hard to assert that there was an ordered three-fold ministry, as now exists in the Catholic Church, in the earliest churches, even though the Preface to the Church of England's Ordination Service says there was ('It is evident unto all men diligently reading Holy Scripture and ancient Authors ... that from the Apostles' time there have been these Orders of Ministers in Christ's Church: Bishops, Priests, and Deacons'); and it is just intellectually dishonest to say that we must interpret the evidence as if this were not so because that is what Christian tradition requires. Reading texts is not that kind of exercise. Insisting on reading James as if it taught justification by faith in the Lutheran sense would be another example of desperately trying to keep the Bible on board when it clearly disagrees with something one holds dear. Luther's reaction, extreme as it was, is more honest: he simply thought James was deficient from this point of view and so rejected it.

This is not to say that the Bible is packed full or error, inconsistency, irrelevance, and self-contradiction. It is, by and large, a profound book, not grossly defective in those ways. But it is profound *literature*, not a creed or confession or set of definitions, and such a work is never going to measure up to the kind of perfections that many religious readers would like to find in it. It is flawed and imperfect, if we regard it as a kind of doctrinal standard. If anyone is to assert, as most Jews and Christians would, that it is the book God wants us to have, then they have to accept that what he wants us to have is this kind of book, *not* a doctrinal standard. When God communicates with the human race, this implies, he communicates in the kinds of way the Bible uses, rather than with a textbook free from all defects and insufficiencies. How did Jesus himself teach, after all? Through parables and riddles and hints and questions, rather than through doctrinal definitions and hard-and-fast rulings. The result is a Bible that is baggy and complex, rather than neat and tidy, and it may be a theological imperative *not* to try to iron it out and make it smooth.

THE BIBLE AS A CULTURAL ARTEFACT

By far the majority of Bible readers, as I began by observing, have a religious agenda and take something like the principles outlined in the first section for granted. Critical readers are in a minority, though in academic biblical study they have come to dominate the field, and the rest of this book will work with the assumption that critical questions are the right ones to ask. But because the Bible has been so deeply influential in Western culture, there are also non-religious readers, largely uninterested in biblical criticism, to whom it is nevertheless important. Very strikingly, Richard Dawkins, who is an enthusiastic apostle of atheism, often speaks warmly of the Bible as a work of beauty and power, especially in the Authorized (King James) Version, and draws on it for the title of one of his books (*River out of Eden: A Darwinian View of Life*, London: Phoenix, 1995). The Bible thus resonates with many people who are indifferent or even hostile to its religious message. The literary critic Northrop Frye expressed it like this: 'this huge, sprawling, tactless book sit[s] there inscrutably in the middle of our cultural heritage, frustrating all our efforts to walk around it' (Northrop Frye, *The Great Code: The Bible and Literature*, London: Routledge & Kegan Paul, 1982, pp. xviii–xix). Many biblical sayings are part of everyone's culture in the West: 'the skin of our teeth', 'no room

at the inn', 'pride goes before a fall'. Most people know at once
what is meant by a 'David and Goliath' contest, and will recognize
allusions to the Garden of Eden, the snake, and the apple (not
explicitly called such in the Bible, but a long-standing element in
Christian reading of Genesis).

LITERARY INFLUENCE

No one can read Western literature intelligently without some
knowledge of the Bible. I have an edition of John Milton's *Paradise
Lost*, for example, in which footnotes referring the reader to biblical
parallels and allusions often take up half the page. In modern times,
Philip Pullman's trilogy *His Dark Materials* draws on both Milton and
his biblical sources, retelling the story of the 'Fall' but treating it as a
positive rather than negative event. The whole effect of this would be
lost on anyone who did not know the Eden story, and there are
probably many of Pullman's young readers on whom it is lost. Not
on militant Christian groups, however, who have protested against
both the novels and the film as putting forward atheist propaganda.

RECEPTION HISTORY

In the academic world there has recently been a boom in studies of
the 'reception history' of the Bible, just as there has of the reception
of Shakespeare, for example. Scholars now regularly ask what generations of readers have 'made' of the biblical books – especially the
narrative ones such as Genesis, the books of Judges or Samuel, and
the Gospels—rather than only asking what the books 'originally
meant'. Art historians have similarly been interested in the reception of biblical narratives, as could be clearly seen in the National
Gallery's 2000 exhibition 'Seeing Salvation'.

POLITICAL INFLUENCE

The Bible (read without critical questioning) has also been
immensely influential in the political sphere. In the past it was often
used to support conservative political attitudes. For example, much
of the theory underlying the 'divine right of kings' espoused by the
Stuart monarchs in England came from the Bible, especially books

such as Samuel and Kings. Even though the theory foundered, Handel's coronation anthem 'Zadok the priest and Nathan the prophet anointed Solomon king over Israel' is a clear example of using the authority of biblical texts to underpin a positive attitude towards the monarchy. In the USA, where monarchic texts have of course not resonated, conservative forces still appeal to the Bible to support an ideology of individual freedom married to a strong government, and of American 'exceptionalism' and nationalism. Most striking of all is the interest in apocalyptic texts, especially the book of Revelation. Revelation is read as predicting the world in which we live today, and is a central part of the culture of some neo-conservatives, who look for a climax to world history in which forces hostile to America will be defeated and a new world-order instigated. Unlike the Christian Zionism in America discussed above, this vision is not restricted to the very religious, but is part of a wider culture.

On the other hand, the Bible has also been used to support not the power of the dominant but the helplessness of the poor and downtrodden, and to offer them hope and empowerment. This has been the case in liberation theology, in which the Bible—especially the stories of the exodus of the Israelites from Egypt—has resonated strongly. A critical reading of Exodus would probably emphasize the creation of nationhood that was to be the climax of the events described there, and would note that it is a contest between Egyptians and Israelites. Liberation theologians, however, have construed it as a contest between the powerful (ruling Egyptians) and the powerless (Israelite slaves), and have taken it as a kind of icon for the empowerment of the poor everywhere, especially of course in Latin America. Again, this has not been of interest only to religious readers of the Bible, but to all concerned with the plight of the downtrodden.

One important consequence of the liberationist use of the Bible was that people sensitized to the theme of liberation then started to question some critical conclusions. Whereas the Bible presents Israel as having entered into the land of Palestine by force of arms, a liberationist perspective sees the Israelites as the poor and weak among the indigenous inhabitants of Palestine, not as a powerful invading army. This picture produces a reconception of the biblical stories in which the Israelite slaves were not really oppressed by Egyptian overlords at all, but were lower class Canaanites, actually native inhabitants of the land of Israel, who rebelled against their over-lords. The exodus story was essentially a myth, casting oppressors and oppressed as belonging to different national or ethnic groups, when originally the contrast had been one of social class. Thus a broadly Marxist analysis of the situation has led many to a radical revision of how the biblical stories should be understood. One of the important 'morals' of this development is that no reading of the Bible exists in a cultural vacuum: King Charles I noticed strands in the biblical history that emphasized the rights of the monarch, ignoring the strong anti-monarchic emphasis also present in 1 Samuel (in chapter 12, for example); while liberation theologians saw the biblical story's potential for inspiring those oppressed by others. In both cases the new perspective had the potential to lead to a different reading of the text, and in the liberationist case actually resulted in new *critical* readings, with a radically new way of thinking about early Israel. Remarkably, recent archaeological work in Israel strongly supports the idea that the Israelites were indigenous to the land, rather than incomers, so that a conclusion originally driven by ideology now turns out to be at least partly justified on strictly historical grounds.

FURTHER READING

John Barton, *What is the Bible?* London: SPCK, 2009 (third edition), offers a basic introduction to the Bible for the general reader. For an introduction that integrates a religious understanding with critical reading see John Muddiman, *The Bible: Fountain and Well of Truth*, Oxford: Basil Blackwell, 1983.

There are discussions of the two approaches outlined in this chapter in John Barton, *The Nature of Biblical Criticism*, Louisville, Ky. and London: Westminster John Knox, 2007. An excellent presentation of the case for a 'committed' reading is made in R. W. L. Moberly, *The Bible, Theology, and Faith: A Study of Abraham and Jesus*, Cambridge: Cambridge University Press, 2000: see also Francis Watson, *Text, Church and World: Biblical Interpretation in Theological Perspective*, Edinburgh: T & T Clark, 1994, and Markus Bockmuehl, *Seeing the Word: Refocusing New Testament Study*, Grand Rapids, Mich.: Baker Academic, 2006.

The title of this chapter is borrowed from the classic study by James Barr, *The Bible in the Modern World*, London: SCM, 1973, which is still worth reading for an overall survey of many of the issues raised here.

2

THE NATURE OF THE BIBLE

THE BIBLICAL CANON

It is usual to refer to the official listing of biblical books as the *canon*, and we may say that Judaism, the Catholic Church, and Protestants have different biblical canons. If you buy an English translation of the Bible it may come in one of three forms. The New Testament section will be identical in all cases, but the much longer section or sections that precede it may differ. First, in most Bibles produced for the use of Protestants, there is only one such section, called 'Old Testament'. But some, second, will also contain the 'Apocrypha' between the two Testaments. And third, in Bibles produced for Catholics, there is no Apocrypha section but most of the books that Protestants call the Apocrypha are to be found integrated within the Old Testament; they are referred to technically as the 'deuterocanonical' books (meaning that in theory they have a somewhat lower status than the other books), but in practice they are treated as equally belonging to the Old Testament. Protestants, however, regard the Apocrypha as definitely less authoritative than the Old and New Testaments, and some (especially Calvinists) reject the Apocrypha altogether, while others (especially Lutherans and Anglicans) treat them as important, though not as so important as the canonical books. (See the chart on pp. 28–9 for the details of all this.)

Thus 'the nature of the Bible' is a more complicated matter than it looks. Furthermore, in Judaism only the books which Protestants call the Old Testament are regarded as sacred: neither the Apocrypha nor (of course) the New Testament is accorded any scriptural status. But there is also a problem about what the books accepted in Judaism should be called. In ancient times they were known simply as 'the books', or sometimes 'the holy books'. Nowadays they are sometimes known by the titles of the three big sections into which Jewish Bibles are divided: the Law (the Pentateuch or books of Moses, Genesis–Deuteronomy); the Prophets (the remaining historical books—Joshua, Judges Samuel, Kings plus the books of prophets such as Isaiah, Jeremiah, Amos); and the Writings (everything else, including Psalms, Proverbs, Ruth, and a number of other books). In Hebrew these titles are Torah, Neviim, and Ketuvim, and the initial letters are sometimes made into the acronym Tanakh or Tenakh. But in English-speaking culture Jews tend generally to speak of the books simply as 'the Bible', and in Israel people who teach biblical studies in universities are usually called Professors 'of Bible'.

'OLD TESTAMENT' OR 'HEBREW BIBLE'?

The question arises what the 'Old Testament' should be called in contexts where Jews and Christians are in dialogue, and in the academic world where there is a desire not to name the books in a way that suggests a religious commitment. The problem with 'Old Testament' is that it seems to some to imply that these books are superannuated by comparison with the 'New Testament', and thus to be at least potentially anti-Semitic. Indeed, the expression 'Old Testament' did originate in circles that thought poorly of Judaism: it is first attested in the writings of Melito of Sardis (who died about AD 190), who draws a contrast between the writings belonging to God's 'new covenant' with Christians and those that belonged to the 'old covenant' with the Jews, which is now superseded ('testament' is simply the Latin for covenant). The general consensus is that to avoid this Christian 'supersessionism' it would be better to call these books 'the Hebrew Bible', and that term has become more or less universal in North American scholarship on the Bible, though the UK lags behind and still has, for example, a Society for Old Testament Study.

While not wanting to express the idea that Christianity has superseded Judaism, it seems to me that the term Hebrew Bible is not too good either. For one thing, not everything in it is in Hebrew! There are sections in Daniel and Ezra that are in Aramaic, a language closely related to Hebrew (about as closely as German is to Dutch), which was the majority language of international diplomacy throughout much of the first millennium BC, far more important than Hebrew, the language only of the land of Israel. For another, the Apocrypha, which all biblical scholars need to study irrespective of its religious status, is not in Hebrew at all, but in Greek, though manuscripts of a Hebrew original have turned up in the case of the book variously called Sirach, The Wisdom of Jesus son of Sira, or Ecclesiasticus (not to be confused with the Old Testament book Ecclesiastes), and also in the case of Tobit. And third, what in that case are we to call the early Christian books normally known as the New Testament? If there is no 'Old Testament', then the title 'New Testament' lacks sense. In the academic world it is sometimes resolved by talking about the study of 'the Hebrew Bible and Christian origins' instead of 'Old and New Testaments'. But in a printed Bible that will not really work. And the 'committed' readers I discussed in chapter 1 will probably feel that such language is rather reductionist, as though these were all 'merely' historical documents rather than books making a faith claim. All in all the issue of nomenclature is very difficult to resolve. 'First' and 'Second Testament' is one possible solution, but one might ask why the word 'Testament' should be used at all. People at large, who are not immersed in biblical study, are likely to go on talking of the Old and New Testaments, and Bibles will certainly go on being produced with those titles in them. In this book 'Hebrew Bible' will generally be preferred despite its shortcomings, but I shall sometimes use 'Old Testament' as the conventional and traditional term, without meaning to imply any particular doctrinal position.

Linked with this usage is the issue of how we express dates. Traditionally in English books dates before the birth of Jesus are indicated using 'BC' ('before Christ'), and dates after it with 'AD' (anno Domini, 'in the year of the Lord'). Some people have thought that both these designations imply an acceptance of Christianity. Of course they do, if one thinks about their original meaning, and the alternatives often used nowadays are 'BCE', 'before the Common Era', and 'CE', 'in the Common Era'. The problem with these latter abbreviations is that they are not widely known to the general public. In this book I have used the older designations, not in order to express any particular religious stance, but simply because they are the abbreviations most people know. I believe that almost no one thinks about the original meaning, but that they are used in common parlance as merely arbitrary signs. As with the use of 'Old Testament', my usage is pragmatic.

ORDER OF THE OLD TESTAMENT BOOKS

Jewish Bibles differ from Christian ones not only in always exclud- ing the Apocrypha, most of whose books are considerably later in origin than books in the Hebrew Bible, but also in the order in which the books are arranged. Christian Bibles, whether or not they include the apocryphal/deuterocanonical books, arrange the books into three categories, which rest on the genre of the books. First come all the narrative or historical books, Genesis to Esther; then what Christians call the didactic or 'wisdom' books, Job, Psalms, Proverbs, Ecclesiastes and the Song of Solomon; then third the prophetic books, starting with the 'major' (i.e. longer) books, Isaiah, Jeremiah, Ezekiel, and Daniel, and concluding with the 'minor' (i.e. shorter) books such as Amos, Hosea, or Haggai. Where the deuterocanonical books are incorporated into the Old Testament, as in Catholic Bibles, they appear next to the books they most resemble: thus the books of Maccabees, which are his- torical, are tacked on after Esther, and the book called the Wisdom of Solomon is placed in the 'wisdom' section.

In Jewish Bibles the arrangement, as spelled out in the preceding section, is also threefold, but the criterion is not generic. It seems likely that it has something to do with the dates at which the var- ious books came to be authoritative. The Torah or Pentateuch is sacred in Judaism to an extent not true even of the other scriptural books, let alone any other writings: in the synagogue it alone is read from one of the scrolls kept in the sacred cupboard or ark, and the reader avoids touching it, using a pointer to keep the place. The Prophets include not only what most people would think of as prophets, named individuals whose utterances have been preserved in books bearing their names, but also the historical books that tell the story of Israel from the death of Moses to the exile to Babylon (Joshua, Judges, Samuel, and Kings). It is not clear why or how these historical books came to be called 'Prophets', though they do contain stories about a number of prophets, such as Elijah and Elisha. The third section of the Hebrew Bible is called simply 'the Writings', which is hardly a title at all, and it contains most of the books that seem to be later in origin than those in the other sections: Chronicles, Daniel, Esther; though it also contains what may well be quite early books, such as Psalms and Proverbs. No one has ever discovered a really satisfactory explanation for the distribution of the books between Prophets and Writings, and in practical terms they have the same kind of status, less by far than the Torah but more or less equal to each other.

THE NEW TESTAMENT

The New Testament canon requires much less comment, because since the fourth century AD at the latest it has been agreed among Christians. Before that time there were disputes about certain books that have never been regarded as central anyway, such as the shorter letters of Peter and John, and occasionally about more major works: in the Eastern churches Revelation was sometimes questioned, in the West the Letter to the Hebrews.

But long before anyone drew up official lists, the four Gospels and the major letters of Paul had an assured status, and were quoted from the second century onwards as absolutely authoritative.

The order of the books is now agreed among Christians, except that some Lutheran Bibles shunt Hebrews, James, Jude, and Revelation into an appendix, since Luther regarded them as of lesser status than the other books. But in the early centuries the order often varied. There were Bibles with the Gospels in various different orders from the one we are familiar with. And whereas Acts now comes between the Gospels and the Letters of Paul, in ancient times it regularly introduced the non-Pauline (or 'Catholic') letters, those of Peter, John, and Jude, probably on the basis that these were disciples of Jesus and hence should precede Paul, who came later to faith. So the earliest complete New Testaments tended to be in four sections: Gospels; Acts + Catholic Letters;

Letters of Paul; Revelation. ('Catholic' here means 'addressed to the whole church', by contrast with Paul's letters, which are to individual communities or people.)

THE TRANSMISSION OF THE BIBLE

How does it come about that we still possess the Old and New Testaments at all, when they were written and compiled so many centuries ago? In a world before printing, this was only because they were continuously copied and recopied by generations of scribes.

THE OLD TESTAMENT

In the case of the Old Testament, there were until recent times no manuscripts copied any earlier than the late first millennium AD, something like a thousand years after the last Old Testament book (Daniel) was written. It was only the discovery of the Dead Sea Scrolls that made available manuscripts going back to the last years BC. The library at Qumran, where the Scrolls were written or at any rate preserved, possessed more than one copy of many Old Testament books, and nearly all the books are represented at least in fragmentary form. It is remarkable how close these manuscripts are, in general, to what had previously been the earliest manuscript, the 'Leningrad Codex' (eleventh century AD), which is the basis for all modern printed Hebrew Bibles. From quite early in the Christian era there seems to have been a tradition of copying very exactly: in the Hebrew Bible even what are obvious mistakes in the text are copied exactly, and there are even marginal notes to remind the scribe not to correct the error!

THE NEW TESTAMENT

Where the New Testament is concerned the manuscript evidence is much nearer the origins of the books, with fragments of New Testament books written on papyrus—mostly from Egypt, where the dry climate preserved them—from as early as the second century AD, not long after the later books of the New Testament (2 Peter, for example) seem to have been written. But there is a striking difference from the Old Testament manuscript tradition: the copying is rarely exact, and there does not seem to have been any insistence that it should be. Scribes varied and corrected the text they were copying. In the case of the Gospels, they often 'harmonized' one Gospel with another. For example, sayings of Jesus that occur in different forms in Matthew and Mark often appear in particular manuscripts of Mark in the Matthaean form, probably because Matthew was read more and so was more familiar. It is not until the fourth century that we find major manuscripts containing the whole of the New Testament, such as the great Codex Sinaiticus, now in the British Library in London. In the New Testament as in the Old the order of books is sometimes different from the one we are used to, reflecting a lack of fixity in the biblical canon.

TEXTUAL CRITICISM

Our modern Bibles rest on decisions about which of the various forms of the biblical text found in manuscripts are more likely to be the oldest, and therefore nearest to what the biblical authors actually wrote. The art of making decisions about this is known as textual criticism. Thus no printed version of either the Old Testament (Hebrew Bible) or New Testament unquestionably reflects what the authors actually wrote. They are all an expert's best guess as to what the original books probably contained. It is worth remembering this when people press very exact verbal details of the biblical text in argument. In broad terms we can feel confident that we have reliable Bibles, but the fine detail—and there is a lot of that—varies a good deal among the available manuscripts, and there is no one completely authoritative version. This is particularly true of the New Testament, and above all of the Gospels, where even in very early times there does not seem to have been even an ideal of a fixed text, let alone the reality of one. The Old Testament in its Hebrew form was more or less fixed by the time of Jesus, though even there the Dead Sea Scrolls show that some books existed in different forms (for example, scrolls of the Psalms have them in different orders); but even the Dead Sea versions are in some cases centuries later than the original books, and there is no knowing what changes may have been introduced over the intervening centuries. We know, for example, that the book of Jeremiah existed in both a longer and a

shorter form, and which (if either!) really goes back to Jeremiah is
an unanswerable question.

A simple example of textual criticism in action is provided by
Psalm 100. Modern translations all render verse 3 so as to say that

Figure 1 Books of the Hebrew and Greek Bibles

The Hebrew Bible

Torah	'Former' Prophets	'Latter' Prophets	Writings
Genesis	Joshua	Isaiah	Psalms
Exodus	Judges	Jeremiah	Job
Leviticus	Samuel	Ezekiel	Proverbs
Numbers	Kings	The Twelve:	Ruth
Deuteronomy		*Hosea*	Song of Songs
		Joel	Ecclesiastes
		Amos	Lamentations
		Obadiah	Esther
		Jonah	Daniel
		Micah	Ezra-Nehemiah
		Nahum	Chronicles
		Habakkuk	
		Zephaniah	
		Haggai	
		Zechariah	
		Malachi	

The Greek Bible

Historical Books	Didactic Books	Prophetic Books
Genesis	Psalms	Twelve Minor Prophets:
Exodus	Proverbs	*Hosea*
Leviticus	Ecclesiastes	*Joel*
Numbers	Song of Songs	*Amos*
Deuteronomy	Job	*Obadiah*
Joshua	Wisdom of Solomon*	*Jonah*
Judges	Ecclesiasticus*	*Micah*
Ruth		*Nahum*
1 Samuel		*Habakkuk*
2 Samuel		*Zephaniah*
1 Kings		*Haggai*
2 Kings		*Zechariah*
1 Chronicles		*Malachi*
2 Chronicles		Isaiah

Figure 1 (continued)
The Greek Bible

1 Esdras	Jeremiah
Ezra	Baruch 1-5*
Nehemiah	Lamentations
Esther	Letter of Jeremiah
(with additions*)	(= Baruch 6)*
Judith*	Ezekiel
Tobit*	Susanna (= Daniel 13)*
1 Maccabees*	Daniel 1-12 (with additions
2 Maccabees*	of Song of Azariah* and
3 Maccabees*	Song of the Three Jews*)
4 Maccabees*	Bel and The Dragon
	(= Daniel 14)*

* Books additional to the Hebrew Bible

God made us 'and we are his', whereas in older versions we read that he made us 'and not we ourselves' (hence the line in the well-known hymn 'All people that on earth do dwell', a metrical version of Psalm 100, that runs, 'without our aid he did us make'). The difference rests on the presence or absence of one letter in the Hebrew original. The received Hebrew text reads *lo' anachnu*, 'not we', but textual critics from ancient times have conjectured that the correct wording is probably *lo anachnu*, omitting the Hebrew letter aleph, represented by the apostrophe. This means 'we to him', that is 'we belong to him', 'we are his'. Which is more likely to be original is a matter of judgement— textual criticism is not scientific. But thinking in ancient Israel probably did not encompass the idea that we might have made ourselves, even to reject it, so in all probability the reading 'we are his' is preferable.

ANCIENT TRANSLATIONS

There are sacred books in the world that have always been known and used only in their original language. This is true, for example, of the Qur'an, never read by Muslims except in Arabic. It is a striking fact that by far the majority of people who have encountered the Hebrew Bible (Old Testament) and Greek New Testament have done so in the form of a translation into another language.

THE TARGUMS

By the time of Jesus many Jews, even in Palestine, were no longer fluent in Hebrew. It had become a religious language, rather like Latin in the Roman Catholic Church, which was no longer spoken by ordinary people. Palestinian Jews mostly spoke Aramaic. Aramaic had been spoken all over the Middle East in the first millennium BC and had served as a means of communication among people who did not know each other's languages, much as English does today. By the first century Greek had supplanted it as the universal language, but it was still spoken by most people in Palestine. So the need arose, if the Bible was to be understood, for it to be translated into Aramaic. The Aramaic translations, which are often quite loose, more paraphrase than strict translation, are known by the Aramaic word *targum* (plural *targumin*), meaning 'interpretation'. They exist for the most important parts of the Hebrew Bible, the Pentateuch and the Prophets, and for some of the Writings.

THE SEPTUAGINT

By the last couple of centuries BC there had arisen a similar development for the Jews outside Palestine, and especially in Egypt, whose everyday language was by now Greek. So Greek versions of the Hebrew Bible began to be produced. There is a legend that the Greek translation of the Pentateuch was made for the Egyptian king Ptolemy Philadelphus (285–246 BC), and that the work was carried out by seventy-two translators who all worked independently yet produced (through divine inspiration) an identical version. Because of this the Greek Old Testament is usually known as the Septuagint (Latin for 'seventy'), abbreviated LXX (Roman numeral for seventy). The Septuagint is deeply important for the history of Christianity, since it is usually this version that New Testament authors, writing in Greek, quote from. Some, including Paul, could undoubtedly read Hebrew, but their everyday Bible was the LXX. In later years the Jewish community turned against the LXX, because it was preserved in Christian circles and at times, they suspected, had been tweaked to make it support Christianity. Further Greek translations, allegedly truer to the Hebrew, were produced by three scholars, Aquila, Symmachus, and Theodotion, parts of whose work still survive. The LXX went on to become *the* Old Testament for the Greek-speaking churches, and remains the official Bible of the Greek Orthodox Church to this day. The LXX contains the deuterocanonical books, and its order is broadly that still encountered in Christian Bibles, with histories, wisdom books, and prophets as the three divisions. At the Reformation in the sixteenth century Protestants came to think that only the books of which there were Hebrew originals should be regarded as fully authoritative, and they shunted the deuterocanonical books into a supplement, the 'Apocrypha', but left the order of the books that remained as it had been in the LXX. Thus the Protestant Old Testament consists of the Jewish Scriptures but in the Christian order—rather an anomaly.

THE VULGATE

In the West, in Western Europe and North Africa, Latin became in due course the language of everyday, and the need for translation arose again. The first Latin version of the Bible—now of the New Testament as well as the Old, since not all Christians could understand the New Testament in Greek—is known as the Old Latin (*Vetus Latina* in Latin). The Old Latin of the Old Testament—which consists of a selection of independent translations into Latin, sometimes several different ones for a given book—was translated not directly from the Hebrew, which hardly any Christians knew, but from the LXX, so it is a translation of a translation. In the fourth century AD St Jerome went to the trouble of learning some Hebrew from Jewish scholars in Palestine, and translated the whole Old Testament from the original. This version was not universally popular with Christians, who clung to the old familiar Vetus Latina, but in time it established itself as the 'common' Latin Bible, in Latin *Biblia Vulgata*. It is known in English as the Vulgate, and remains the official Bible of the Roman Catholic Church, though in modern times it has been revised to form a 'New Vulgate' (*Nova Vulgata*).

MODERN TRANSLATIONS

EARLY MODERN TRANSLATIONS

From about the time of the Reformation in the sixteenth century the Bible began to be translated into the vernacular languages of Europe. There was opposition to this from the officialdom of the Catholic Church, and some people (such as William Tyndale, d. 1536) were even executed for translating the Latin Bible. But, especially with the rise of printing, the process of producing vernacular versions became unstoppable. The German Reformer Martin Luther single-handedly produced a complete translation of the whole Bible into German, an achievement as remarkable as Jerome's. In England there were several revisions of Tyndale's Bible, such as the Bishops' Bible, which preceded the eventual production of what is known in Britain as the Authorized Version (AV) and in America as the King James Version (KJV). This was made under the official auspices of King James I by a panel of scholars, and was published in 1611. As the Preface makes clear, it was a deliberate revision of earlier translations, not a brand-new version:

> we never thought from the beginning, that we should need to make a new Translation, nor yet to make of a bad one a good one ... but to make a good one better, or out of many good ones, one principal good one, not justly to be excepted against; that hath been our endeavour, that our mark.
>
> (Preface, AV)

It established itself as the standard English Bible for the next two and a half centuries, and is still of course widely used and revered today, not least for the excellence of its English style.

MORE RECENT TRANSLATIONS

During the nineteenth century advances in understanding Hebrew and Greek, together with an awareness that there were places where the AV was hopelessly obscure, led to pressure for a revision. Between 1881 and 1895 the Revised Version (RV) was published in

Britain, and an American equivalent, the American Standard Version (ASV), in 1901. These versions are now hard to come by, and from a modern perspective represent only a light revision of the AV.

During the twentieth century there was a fresh development in English Bible translation: versions produced by individuals working from the original languages, and not simply revising existing versions but starting from scratch. Notable examples are those by James Moffat in 1935 and J. B. Phillips (mainly limited to the New Testament) in the 1940s and 1950s. The latter was often arrestingly modern and avoided hallowed phrases—even the titles, such as *Letters to Young Churches* for Paul's Letters and *The Young Church in Action* for the Acts of the Apostles told the reader to expect something with a contemporary idiom.

But most twentieth-century Bibles, like the AV, were the work of committees. There are, however, two distinct traditions.

One works, like the AV itself, by revising earlier versions. Thus the ASV was revised to produce the Revised Standard Version (RSV, completed in 1957), which still has the flavour of the AV but eliminates many archaic phrases and pays conscious attention to the original languages. (This is the translation used in this book.) This tradition continues in the New Revised Standard Version (NRSV), which has established itself as the version of choice for many students of the Bible in the English-speaking world, from all Christian denominations. Its most salient characteristic is the use of 'inclusive language', that is, wherever possible it avoids purely male language where the text implies an audience both male and female (thus Paul's address to his readers as 'brothers' becomes 'brothers and sisters' even though there is no word corresponding to 'sisters' in the text itself). 'Son of man' in Ezekiel similarly becomes 'Mortal'. This makes the Bible less offensive to many readers, but unfortunately also sometimes falsifies what its authors (who were often quite androcentric) actually intended.

The other tradition, following the lead of Moffat and Phillips, starts from scratch. This approach led to the New English Bible (NEB—later revised as the Revised English Bible (REB)), produced by a panel drawn from all the Protestant churches, and the Jerusalem Bible (JB—later revised as the New Jerusalem Bible (NJB)), which followed the lead of the French Bible de Jérusalem, a Catholic version.

Two other important modern translations should be mentioned. Evangelical Christians often use the New International Version (NIV), which has a style not unlike the NRSV (modernized AV), but concentrates on translating various passages where the meaning is disputed in such a way as to favour an evangelical interpretation. The Jewish community for many years used either the AV or modified versions of it (of course only the Old Testament), but now tends to prefer the Jewish Publication Society (JPS) version, which sticks very faithfully to the Hebrew text as it can be found in printed Hebrew Bibles and avoids changing it, as most Christian Bibles (including NIV) do, when it seems to most scholars to contain errors. It is, in effect, the only modern Bible not affected by textual criticism.

ATTITUDES TOWARDS TRANSLATION

Almost all Christians, and many Jews, encounter the Bible only in translation. Some translations have the aim of preserving the tradition of earlier English versions (there are parallels in other modern languages), and thus helping readers to fit into a long Christian history, hearing the same, or nearly the same, words as their forebears in faith. Others set themselves the task of surprising readers and encouraging them to put themselves back in the position of the first believers, hearing the word of God for the first time. In a religion such as Christianity, which is two thousand years old, there can be a valid place for both approaches.

But in neither case can the reader afford to become fixated on one particular version as though it somehow preserved God's word in a definitive form. If there is to be such a feeling at all, it would need to attach to the 'original' Bible, in Hebrew, Aramaic, and Greek, and not to translations into any other language at all. But, as we have seen, even the 'original' Bible is something of an enigma. We do not possess the book of Genesis as it left the hands of its original author, in the way that we can possess the manuscript of a modern writer. The situation is more like our relation to Shakespeare, where there are several different versions of many plays, some or all authorized by him, and some representing the working copies used by actors, so that the 'original' Shakespeare may not only be hard to reconstruct in practice, but actually impossible in principle—there is simply no such thing. The apparent fixity and permanence of the Bible as it shines out from a solid printed translation conceals an enormous amount of diversity and uncertainty that confronts anyone who peeps behind the scenes. This does not mean that there is really no Bible at all: the uncertainties represent only a portion of the whole. But knowing something of how we got our English Bibles it makes it hard to respond in a fundamentalist way to the exact wording that confronts us when we open them.

THE ORIGINS OF THE BIBLE: THE NEW TESTAMENT

So far we have looked at the compilation and the transmission of the various biblical books. But how did they originate? This is a long and complex story. It may be best to begin with the New Testament, which came into being over a much shorter period of time than the Hebrew Bible,

I vividly remember my first meeting with my New Testament teacher when I began to study theology. He said, 'Well, we should begin at the beginning.' So on my fresh pad of paper I wrote: 'Matthew.' 'So,' he went on, 'I'd like you all to write an essay on 1 Thessalonians.' This was one of those moments in which one's understanding of something is changed for ever. What I suddenly realized was that the New Testament was not a flat, two-dimensional work, but one with a history. The earliest stage in that history was not the Gospels, even though they are of course concerned with the earliest *events*, but the letters of St Paul. And furthermore, among those letters the first is not the first one you meet when you leaf through a New Testament, namely Romans, but the first letter to the Thessalonians, hardly most Bible-readers' favourite part of the New Testament. In our New Testaments the Gospels come first because they are the story of Jesus, not because they were written first, and the letters of Paul begin with Romans, not because Romans was the first letter he wrote, but because it's the longest: the letters are simply arranged in descending order of length. But by tracing Paul's career from the book of Acts and correlating it with the various churches he wrote to, you can work out the order in which they were written; and if you do that, you will find that 1 Thessalonians is the earliest letter.

THREE STAGES IN THE GROWTH OF THE NEW TESTAMENT

The New Testament came into being, broadly speaking, in three stages. First, in the 40s and 50s AD, we have the letters of Paul. Paul knew a good deal about Jesus—who after all was his older contemporary—which he had learned from the disciples, although he never gives us a detailed account of Jesus' life; but he knew about the crucifixion and resurrection of course, and he recalls other traditions about Jesus, such as his institution of the Lord's supper or Eucharist.

Second, from about the late 60s onwards writers decided no longer to rely on oral memory for the stories about Jesus, but began to write them down to make what we call the Gospels. Mark was almost certainly the earliest, followed by Matthew, Luke, and John, later ones relying on earlier ones but adding material of their own. The interrelationship of the three 'Synoptic' Gospels, Matthew, Mark, and Luke, is the subject of many very complex theories. The majority view is that Matthew and Luke used Mark but added material from another document, now lost, which explains overlaps between them that do not derive from Mark. This document is traditionally called Q (from the German *Quelle*, 'source'). For various reasons most scholars do not think that Matthew and Luke knew each other's work: consequently the parallels between them can only be explained on the basis of some shared source such as Q. Acts was written to be a second volume of Luke, presumably at about the same time.

Third, overlapping with the writing of the Gospels, the other letters in the New Testament and the book of Revelation took shape—the letters attributed to Peter and John and James. At the same time, and by now we may be in the 90s AD, other letters were written and said to be by Paul, though most New Testament scholars think they are not really by him: examples are Ephesians and the so-called 'Pastoral Epistles', the letters to Timothy and Titus. Some think that Colossians and 2 Thessalonians are also falsely ascribed to Paul.

PSEUDONYMITY

The idea that documents in the New Testament can be pseudonymous—that is, written by someone other than the author they claim to derive from—is scandalous to some people, since it seems to imply that the Bible is lying. This is a complex problem. In ancient times authorship was not defended as much as it is in our age, with its awareness of copyright and plagiarism. On the other hand, presumably the claim that a given letter was by Paul when really it was not was an attempt to give it enhanced authority, and the Pastorals even mention things Paul is supposed to be doing at the time of writing, so that the false attribution is hardly just a literary convention of some kind. There are certainly scholars who still defend the Pauline authorship of the Pastorals—though fewer do the same for the apostolic authorship of letters of Peter and James, even though the same problems of veracity arise there. The whole question of pseudonymity in the New Testament is still unresolved among New Testament scholars.

There is anyway at least one letter that almost no one nowadays thinks is by Paul: the Letter to the Hebrews. Some people in ancient times thought this Pauline, but it never claims to be, even though the AV entitles it 'The Epistle of Paul the Apostle to the Hebrews'. It is in any case hardly a letter, but more like a sermon, and its origins are mysterious, but from its theological stance it too seems to belong in the third period of the composition of New Testament books. There are thus three generations of writings in the New Testament: Paul; Gospels and Acts; pseudo-Paul and other letters.

PLACE OF ORIGIN

Where was the New Testament written? The Christian community began its life in Jerusalem, but, as we learn from Acts, it spread rapidly into other parts of the Roman Empire. One major centre was Antioch in Syria, and it may be there that Matthew, for example, was composed. Asia Minor (modern Turkey) was also very important, having been evangelized by Paul. Some think that the first Gospel, Mark, was written in Rome, where there was a Christian community from early times, not founded by Paul: when he writes to them in the Letter to the Romans he makes it clear that they were not his own converts. Each of Paul's letters is to the Christians in a different city, but there is good reason to think that in the next generation the letters were collected together for the benefit of Christians generally—and Romans seems designed from the beginning to have something of the character of an encyclical for many churches. In the case of the Gospels there is great debate among scholars as to whether each Gospel is intended for one particular community, or whether the Gospels were from the beginning meant to be for all the churches. (This question is discussed further in the next chapter.)

On the one hand each has a particular flavour that might be characteristic of one church. Mark contains a few Latin words, and seems to know the situation in Rome, and in the sayings of Jesus about divorce the Marcan version envisages the possibility that a woman might divorce her husband, which was allowed in Roman but not in Jewish law. Matthew greatly emphasizes the difference between Christianity and Judaism, and perhaps reflects a community which had to mark itself out from its Jewish compatriots, maybe more necessary in Syria than in some other places in the Roman Empire. John shows a familiarity with popular Greek philosophy (for example, in his Prologue about the 'Word' of God becoming incarnate in Jesus), and this might suggest an origin in Alexandria in Egypt, where such philosophy was more developed than elsewhere.

But on the other hand, each Gospel seems intended to supersede earlier ones, as though Gospels were meant for all Christians. Matthew is a reworking of Mark; Luke explicitly tells us in its prologue that the author had studied other lives of Jesus and wished to provide a definitive version (see Luke 1:1–4); and John tells such a different story that it is hard to think of it as meant to stand alongside the others as merely one local version of the gospel: it looks like an attempt to replace the other Gospels with a radically different version of the life of Jesus. It is rather extraordinary that such different accounts of Jesus came into being over a comparatively short period, maybe about thirty years from the 60s to the 90s AD. The early Christian movement was a variegated phenomenon, and the New Testament bears witness to its variety rather than to its unity.

THE ORIGINS OF THE BIBLE: HEBREW BIBLE

The origins of the Hebrew Bible/Old Testament could hardly be more different from those of the New Testament. Traditionally biblical scholars have thought of the Hebrew Bible as spanning a period close to a thousand years, from the earliest poems (possibly the Song of Moses in Exodus 15 and the Song of Deborah in Judges 5) in the tenth or eleventh century BC to Daniel in the second century BC and, if we include the Apocrypha, Sirach in the second half of the second century BC and the Wisdom of Solomon in the first century BC. The trend in recent scholarship is to be sceptical about the possibility of texts coming from quite so early as used to be thought: for example, in the Song of Moses, though it celebrates the exodus and the crossing of the Red Sea in the time of Moses (possibly in the thirteenth century), there are references to the temple in Jerusalem, so that the Song cannot, at least in its present form, be older than the building of the temple. The temple is said in the Bible to have been built by Solomon (tenth century), but some people now suspect that it was constructed even later than that, and attributed to Solomon fictitiously. Nevertheless, the time covered by the writing of the Hebrew Bible is certainly much longer than that covered by the New Testament.

THREE STAGES IN COMPOSITION OF NARRATIVE BOOKS

But without forcing the parallel, it may be said that at least the narrative books of the Hebrew Bible (which make up at least half of the whole) also developed in three waves. Most scholars continue to think that there was a major explosion of writing in the years before the Babylonian Exile of the sixth century BC. In older scholarship it was customary to think that the age of David and Solomon (tenth century) was a period of massive cultural expansion—it was some-times referred to as 'the Solomonic Enlightenment'. Recent archae-ology has suggested that Jerusalem, where David and Solomon are supposed to have ruled, could not have supported such a movement so early, and we tend now to think of the eighth century, the age of King Hezekiah and of the prophet Isaiah, as the period when the writing of narrative took off. Much in the historical books, and especially the books of Samuel, could well come from this period. They are written in a flowing Hebrew style and contain many well-told stories, such as the story of David and Bathsheba (2 Samuel 11). There may well be material in Joshua and Judges that also stems from this period, often drawing on oral tradition about the heroes and villains of the past. Perhaps even more important, there are strands in the Pentateuch that make sense against the background of pre-exilic Israel and Judah, including many of the stories of Abraham, Isaac, and Jacob, and the life of Moses. These stories are unlikely to preserve accurate memories of the heroes whose lives they narrate, but on the other hand they are equally unlikely to be pure fictitious compositions: they contain folk-memories worked up with great literary skill into complex narrative texts, and they probably antedate the Exile of the sixth century BC.

Second, the time of the Exile itself (586–530 BC) seems to have been a major stimulus to writing. It is from this time, most scholars think, that the completed version of all the historical books from Joshua to Kings derives, incorporating the earlier books such as Samuel but reshaping the whole history of Israel to show how it ended in defeat and exile. This finished work is often known nowadays as the Deuteronomistic History, because it judges the rulers of Israel and Judah in the light of legislation found in the book of Deuteronomy. There may have been a pre-exilic edition of the History, but few doubt that it was the Exile that gave it its present character as an elegiac work mourning the downfall of the nation.

Third, a lot of Hebrew narrative was compiled or composed in the years after the Exile, when the Jews lived under the Persian Empire. This is the age that produced the books of Chronicles, Ezra and Nehemiah, which continue the story told in the Deuteronomistic History down into post-exilic times. It also saw the formulation of other strands in the Pentateuch and the final editing of that work into the form we now have. And it was in the Persian period that the stories of Job, Esther, and Ruth were probably written.

OTHER BOOKS

If we take this broad outline as a basis for dating other Hebrew books, the long-standing consensus has been that parts at least of the books of Deuteronomy, Proverbs, and the Psalms go back into pre-exilic times, and were formulated at the same time as the great early narrative books were being written, during the flowering of the monarchy in the two kingdoms of Israel and Judah. The other major works from the period are the books of the most important prophets, such as Amos, Hosea, Micah, Isaiah, and Jeremiah. All the prophetic books have been heavily edited and re-edited over a long period, and there are indeed very few books in the Hebrew Bible of which this is not true. But a basic core does go back to the prophets whose names the books bear, and sometimes we can reconstruct this core.

The exilic age saw the production not only of the Deuteronomistic History but also of the important short book, Lamentations, which is a dirge over the fall of Jerusalem to the Babylonian army. A few Psalms, especially 74 and 79, fit well in the same period and share many themes with Lamentations. Also from the exilic age come two major prophetic works: the book of Ezekiel, and the prophecies by an anonymous figure that appear in Isaiah 40–55, usually referred to as Deutero-Isaiah or Second Isaiah.

In the Persian period prophecy continues in the persons of Haggai and Zechariah, and another collection in the book of Isaiah, Trito- or Third Isaiah (Isaiah 56–66). But the major work from post-exilic times is a collection of legal material now located in the Pentateuch, conventionally called the Priestly Work or P. This is an immense collection of detailed legislation, mostly about matters of ritual, which has been interwoven with the early narratives that were the earlier substratum of Genesis–Numbers to produce the strange mix of legislation and stories that is so characteristic of the Pentateuch. Nowadays the study of the Pentateuch tends to dis-tinguish just these two main strands, P and 'non-P', but earlier scholars differentiated 'non-P' into three distinct sources, the earliest being J—so-called because it holds that God was called by his spe-cial name Yahweh (Jahwe in German) from the earliest times; the second-oldest E, which calls God by the generic name Elohim until the time of Moses; and D, the book of Deuteronomy and a few fragments in the earlier books of the Pentateuch that reflect the same attitudes as Deuteronomy. The intricacy of weaving together four separate strands to make a single work, however, would be immense, and more recently there has been a tendency to simplify the picture and to think essentially of just the two main sources (P and non-P), however much the final edition of the Pentateuch may have been touched up and revised over time.

It is clear that there are few books in the Hebrew Bible that were written continuously at a sitting; nearly all of them are highly com-posite works, resulting from copying and recopying, each time incorporating more material and producing works that are broadly coherent but do not have the degree of unity modern readers expect in a book. Often the editors seem to have wanted to make sure nothing that had come down to them was lost, even though the result left some loose ends. (Strangely enough, however, it is from the post-exilic period that we have Ruth and Esther, as mentioned above, and these are coherent, one-author works.) The post-exilic age also saw the compilation of the book of Psalms and the production of several 'wisdom' books: Proverbs in its final form, Ecclesiastes (known in Hebrew as Qoheleth), and the deuterocanonical works Sirach (Ecclesiasticus) and the Wisdom of Solomon.

What has just been set out is a consensus view of how we came to have the Hebrew Bible. Not all scholars would share it. There are some who still think much more of the Hebrew Bible is earlier than the consensus allows—that P, for example, is pre-exilic, or that the stories of the patriarchs (Abraham, Isaac, and Jacob) and the accounts of Moses genuinely go back to the early period in which they are set (the second millennium BC). Some of these scholars are biblical conservatives who derive their belief in the early date of the biblical books from the fact that these books seem to *claim* to be very old, and who think that the authority of Scripture thus requires us to think they are. (This would correspond to the belief in the case of the Gospels that we are dealing with eyewitness testimony and hence that the Gospels go back into the age of Paul, in the 40s or 50s AD.) This is not uniformly true, however, and the belief that P is early is very common among Jewish scholars, without their being in any sense fundamentalist or ultra-conservative.

LATE DATINGS

Probably more influential at present, however, is the opposite view: that the consensus dates many books too early. An important school of thought holds that almost all the writings in the Hebrew Bible are the product of the Persian period, or even more extremely of the Hellenistic age that followed the conquest of Persia by Alexander the Great in the 300s BC. On such a view not only Chronicles but also Kings, on which it rests, came into being well after the Exile; and the stories of David, Solomon, Hezekiah, Elijah and Elisha, and even the stories in Genesis and Exodus, are all

fictions produced in the fifth or fourth century BC and simply projected back into a mythical past. What is more, on this understanding the prophetic books are also late, not only in their final
form (which most would agree) but even in their core elements:
they have no connection with the prophets whose names they bear,
these also being fictitious characters.

Such a view, currently known as 'minimalist', has implications
not only for what we can know about written sources in pre-exilic
times (basically, that there weren't any), but also about what we can
reconstruct of the early history of Israel. If there are no written
sources until after the exile, then what preceded it is bound to be
very misty. At the same time, minimalism stresses how little we can
know historically about early Israel. No evidence has turned up for
the reigns of the early kings of Israel and Judah, and if there was
indeed a 'Solomonic Enlightenment' it took place in a tiny city
with a very small population, which is what archaeology reveals
Jerusalem to have been before the eighth century. It is much like-
lier that the age of Solomon is a back-projection from later times.
Fifty years ago biblical historians were confident that many of the
stories in the Pentateuch and the Deuteronomistic History rested
on a solid historical foundation; nowadays more and more scholars
are coming to think that much of the Hebrew Bible is fiction. To
me the extremely detailed and circumstantial accounts of, for
example, the court of David in 2 Samuel seem rather unlikely to be
cut from whole cloth, and I would assume that they do rest on
some historical memory, however garbled. But the belief that the
first of our three periods produced no literature at all is gaining
ground in Old Testament studies at the moment.

NON-CANONICAL LITERATURE

People sometimes ask whether the Bible represents the whole
library of ancient Jewish and Christian works, or is only a selection
from a much larger pool. Both Jews and Christians certainly knew
other written texts, in the form of legal contracts and commercial
documents. But so far as conscious literature is concerned, what we
have in the Bible represents more than merely a small selection of
what was available, so far as we are able to tell. It comprises the
main bulk of what we know later writers referred to as scripture.

OLD TESTAMENT APOCRYPHA AND PSEUDEPIGRAPHA

In the case of the Hebrew Bible, there were a few books that later rabbis cited with a suggestion at least that they had some authority, the main example being Sirach; though from well into the Christian era there are rabbinic discussions that make it clear the book was not put on a par with the Bible. Rabbinic Judaism is not however the only variety of Judaism that existed around the turn of the era, and there is good evidence that other Jews did prize highly works that are not now in the canon that the rabbis recognized. The community at Qumran valued the Temple Scroll, which is a kind of improved and more consistent version of the legal material in the Pentateuch, and also the *Book of Jubilees*, a retelling of the book of Genesis by an angel. Interestingly however both works are in a sense parasitic on material that is already in the Hebrew Bible. There were also many works attributed to other biblical figures, such as Enoch, Adam and Eve, Ezra, and the prophets, which some groups undoubtedly took very seriously and treated as scriptural. After Judaism turned its back on such 'pseudepigraphical' material (writings falsely attributed), many of these works were preserved mainly by Christians, often in translations into remote languages such as Ethiopic (the *Book of Enoch* is still part of the Ethiopian Christian Bible), Armenian, or Slavonic. But for most Christians they did not attain to scriptural status.

NEW TESTAMENT APOCRYPHA

Where the New Testament is concerned, the edges of the canon are also fuzzy. Significant manuscripts such as Codex Sinaiticus include the *Epistle of Barnabas* or the *Shepherd*, by Hermas, alongside the canonical New Testament books, without any suggestion that they are not part of the canon. But even so Christian writers from earliest times allude much less to such works than to the books that would become canonical. Many non-canonical works are manifestly from a later date than even the latest of the New Testament books, and they often derive from what are called 'gnostic' sources. Gnosticism is a hard movement to define, and there is dispute over whether it represents simply a divergent strand of Christianity, which was later suppressed, or was a coherent religio-philosophical movement in its own right, which appealed to some Christians. It stressed the importance of secret knowledge (in Greek *gnosis*) as bringing salvation, and it was often deeply antagonistic to the body, practising extreme asceticism (or, paradoxically, extreme self-indulgence, on the basis that the body didn't matter anyway).

Some Christian/Gnostic works have made headlines in recent years: the *Gospel of Mary Magdalene*, for example, and the *Gospel of Judas*. Dan Brown, in his novel *The Da Vinci Code*, has constructed a theory that these works and others like them were really ancient and that the Church suppressed them in the interests of its own emerging orthodoxy—otherwise they would have got into the New Testament. But this overlooks the late origin of all the non-canonical Gospels: they were never candidates for inclusion in the New Testament anyway, since its contents were pretty well determined by the mid-second century. The evidence for this is not the official lists of canonical books, which start to appear only in the fourth century, but the actual use made of various books by Christian writers. Overwhelmingly they cite the books that we now know as the New Testament. A conspiracy theory about the canon has to argue not simply that later figures who drew up lists of the New Testament books, such as Athanasius, bishop of Alexandria (*c*.296–373), deliberately suppressed these works, but that the vast majority of early Christian writers did so too. This doesn't stand up to examination.

There is probably only one non-canonical work in which scholars have detected possible early material, and that is the *Gospel of Thomas*. This work was discovered at Nag Hammadi in Egypt in 1945–46. It is in Coptic, but is a translation of a Greek original perhaps as old as AD 150, and it consists simply of sayings of Jesus without any narrative—possibly like 'Q', the hypothetical document underlying Matthew and Luke. And some think that it does preserve a few genuine sayings of Jesus; if so, it is almost the only source outside the Gospels that does so. (A few early Christian writers record sayings not exactly the same as those in the Gospels, or little details of incidents in Jesus' life such as what he made in his carpenter's shop.) But the pickings are very thin indeed, and for practical purposes it makes hardly any difference to our knowledge of Jesus and his teachings.

NOTE: THE NAME OF GOD

In the Hebrew Bible the God of Israel has a proper name, just like the gods of other nations. This appears in the Hebrew text as YHWH. We do not know how the name was pronounced in ancient times, but on the basis of some evidence from Greek sources, it may have been Yahweh, and that is the word used for it in this book. The problem arises because Hebrew in ancient times was written with no vowels: the vowels were added much later in the form of various dots and lines, rather like the dots used in shorthand. In the case of most words the later vowels naturally reflect how the words were in fact pronounced, and they rest on very ancient tradition. But by the time the vowels were added, the custom had grown up of not pronouncing the divine name at all, but of saying instead the word for 'lord', in Hebrew 'Adonai'; and so the vowels of Adonai were added to the consonants YHWH. If one tries to pronounce the resulting word, it comes out as Yehowah, which is the origin of the form Jehovah. But pronouncing the name like this is a later Christian practice; the name Jehovah never existed in Judaism. The vowels are simply a reminder to the reader that when YHWH is in the text, the word Adonai is to be read instead. (Modern Orthodox Judaism does not even say Adonai, but 'Hashem', Hebrew for 'the name'.) Biblical translators in ancient times followed Jewish practice, rendering YHWH as *Kurios* in Greek and 'Dominus' in Latin, both meaning 'Lord', and English translations use the same convention but print the word 'Lord' in a distinctive way: LORD, using small capitals for the last three letters. When this form occurs in a biblical translation, you can be sure that YHWH stands in the Hebrew; where 'Lord' is printed in the usual way, then the word 'Adonai' is actually present in the Hebrew text, not YHWH.

The use of the word 'Yahweh' is unacceptable to some Jews, who regard actually saying or writing the divine name as blasphemous, but scholarly convention allows it in books of this kind. Quite often, however, out of respect for Jewish thinking, the name is written 'unvocalized' (i.e. without vowels), as YHWH. The reconstructed pronunciation is not uncontroversial: there is a lot of ancient evidence suggesting that the name may have been pronounced 'Yahoo' or 'Yaho', and it is noticeable that personal names in Hebrew that end in the divine name generally preserve a spelling suggesting that pronunciation—for example, 'Isaiah' in Hebrew is Yesha'yahu, 'Yahu is my salvation'.

FURTHER READING

A basic guide to the development of the Bible is provided by John Barton, *Making the Christian Bible*, London: Darton, Longman & Todd, 1997 (American edition *How the Bible Came to Be*, Louisville, Ky.: Westminster John Knox, 1997).

On the Old Testament canon the relevant material is usefully collected together in Roger Beckwith, *The Old Testament Canon of the New Testament Church and its Background in Early Judaism*, Grand Rapids, Mich.: Eerdmans, 1986, though the interpretation of the evidence is highly conservative and traditional. For the account presented in this chapter see John Barton, *Oracles of God: Perceptions of Ancient Prophecy in Israel after the Exile*, London: Darton, Longman & Todd, 1986.

On the New Testament canon the standard work is Bruce M. Metzger, *The New Testament Canon: Its Origin, Development, and Significance*, Oxford: Clarendon Press, 1987. See also John Barton, *The Spirit and the Letter: Studies in the Biblical Canon*, London: SPCK, 1998 (American edition *Holy Writings, Sacred Text: The Canon in Early Christianity*, Louisville, Ky.: Westminster John Knox, 1998).

There is a good account of the development of the biblical canon and of the ancient translations in *The Cambridge History of the Bible*, vol. 2, Cambridge: Cambridge University Press, 1963–70; a new edition is in preparation. On modern translations see Bruce M. Metzger, *The Bible in Translation: Ancient and English Versions*, Grand Rapids, Mich.: Baker Academic, 2001. A readable account of modern translations is provided by Leonard Greenspoon, 'Jewish Bible Translation' and Henry Wansbrough, 'Christian Bible Translation', both in John Barton (ed.), *The Biblical World*, vol 2, London and New York: Routledge, 2002.

There are several collections of apocryphal works, but one of the most accessible is J. R. Porter, *The Lost Bible: Forgotten Scriptures Revealed*, London: Duncan Baird Publishers, 2001.

Several websites provide good information and excellent links. See especially:

http://www.sots.ac.uk/resources.html

http://www.ntgateway.com/

http://www.theoldtestament.co.uk

3

MAJOR GENRES

The Bible is not only a library of books, it is a library of different *kinds* of book. In this chapter we examine the main genres to which biblical books belong, few of which correspond to anything in modern literature.

NARRATIVE

More than half of the Bible consists of narrative. Often people talk of the 'historical' books of the Hebrew Bible, and it is also common to treat the Gospels and the Acts of the Apostles as historiographical in character. As we saw in the previous chapter, many Old Testament scholars are now coming to see the 'histories' in the Old Testament as containing a good deal of fiction; and the question of history in the Gospels is a very vexed one, and will be examined below. So the term 'narrative', being more neutral, is probably a better one to use of the books from Genesis to Esther in the Hebrew Bible and of the Gospels and Acts in the New Testament.

So much of the Hebrew Bible is narrative that we might regard this as the most characteristic genre in ancient Israel. This is striking, given the background in the ancient Near East. Kings in Mesopotamia kept annals, and it seems from references scattered in Kings that this is true also of the kings of Israel and Judah. And there are myths and legends from both Mesopotamia and Egypt, some of them close to Hebrew stories, and mostly in verse. But nothing like the lengthy and detailed *prose* narratives of the Hebrew Bible has been found in other cultures, and certainly nothing that sets out to convey the whole of recorded time, as the narrative that runs from Genesis to Esther does. There are creation epics in Assyrian and Babylonian culture, one of which, the *Enuma elish*, exists in many copies and was obviously of central importance for those cultures. But they are not connected with the rest of human history, as is the creation story in Genesis 1–2. Hebrew culture seems to have been unusual in the place it gave to continuous accounts of its own past, all more or less harmonized and made to fit into an overall pattern. What is more, at the level of the final editing of the Hebrew Bible there is even a consistent chronology, from which it is possible to calculate the age of the world and to fit every decisive event into its correct year. The chronology probably arose mainly in post-exilic times, when the Pentateuch and the other narrative books were being edited, though there is an underlying record of the regnal years of the kings of Israel and Judah, which probably goes back to court annals.

Three points may be made about the Hebrew narrative books: that they are widely diverse in kind, but people in ancient Israel seem not to have registered this; that they have other genres embedded within them; and that although they record the past, their intended function is probably orientated towards the future.

TYPES OF NARRATIVE

First, Hebrew narrative exhibits a wide variety of what may be called sub-genres. The books of Kings contain a lot of material close to what we might think of as historiography, and which is probably excerpted from royal annals and other official accounts. An example would be this:

> In the fourteenth year of King Hezekiah Sennacherib king of Assyria came up against all the fortified cities of Judah and took them. And Hezekiah king of Judah sent to the king of Assyria at Lachish, saying, 'I have done wrong; withdraw from me; whatever you impose on me I will

bear.' And the king of Assyria required of Hezekiah king of Judah three hundred talents of silver and thirty talents of gold.

(2 Kings 18:13–14)

But they also contain the stories about Elijah and Elisha, and these are surely closer to folktale or legend, often containing accounts of miraculous events, and exhibiting folkloristic patterning, as in this story:

The messengers returned to the king, and he said to them, 'Why have you returned?' And they said to him, 'There came a man to meet us, and said to us, "Go back to the king who sent you, and say to him, Thus says the LORD, Is it because there is no God in Israel that you are sending to inquire of Ba'al-zebub, the god of Ekron? Therefore you shall not come down from the bed to which you have gone, but shall surely die."' He said to them, 'What kind of man was he who came to meet you and told you these things?' They answered him, 'He wore a garment of haircloth, with a girdle of leather about his loins.' And he said, 'It is Elijah the Tishbite.'

Then the king sent to him a captain of fifty men with his fifty. He went up to Elijah, who was sitting on the top of a hill, and said to him, 'O man of God, the king says, "Come down."' But Elijah answered the captain of fifty, 'If I am a man of God, let fire come down from heaven and consume you and your fifty.' Then fire came down from heaven, and consumed him and his fifty.

Again the king sent to him another captain of fifty men with his fifty. And he went up and said to him, 'O man of God, this is the king's order, "Come down quickly!"' But Elijah answered them, 'If I am a man of God, let fire come down from heaven and consume you and your fifty.' Then the fire of God came down from heaven and consumed him and his fifty.

Again the king sent the captain of a third fifty with his fifty. And the third captain of fifty went up, and came and fell on his knees before Elijah, and entreated him, 'O man of God, I pray you, let my life, and the life of these fifty servants of yours, be precious in your sight. Lo, fire came down from heaven, and consumed the two former captains of fifty men with their fifties; but now let my life be precious in your sight.' Then the angel of the LORD said to Elijah, 'Go down with him; do not be afraid of him.' So he arose and went down with him to the king.

(2 Kings 1:5–15)

The pattern of 2 + 1 in the incidents here, with the third differing from the other two, and the 'fire from heaven' element, mark this tale out as having much in common with the folklore of many nations. It may not be real folklore—it could simply be constructed on a traditional pattern. But it is certainly very different from what one would find in an official record.

By contrast, the stories at the beginning of Genesis concerning the creation of the world and of humankind are more like myth, and they are paralleled in myths from other cultures. And some of the later books, such as Ruth, Esther, and Daniel, may be deliberate and conscious fiction, and are sometimes referred to nowadays as 'Jewish novels'. From a modern perspective the narrative material in the Hebrew Bible is thus very diverse.

But almost more important than the fact of its diversity is the observation that no one in Hebrew culture seems to have noticed it. The chronological scheme is in itself evidence of this: the mythical events in the garden of Eden, the legendary exploits of the heroes of early Israel, and the historical victories or defeats of the kings of the two Hebrew kingdoms are all threaded out on a single timeline, without any apparent awareness that they are stories of different *kinds*. In later times, as still today by more conservative readers of the Bible, they are all regarded as 'history' in the same sense: an entirely accurate record of past events, in which people said exactly the things they are alleged to have said and did exactly what they are recorded as doing. People did see problems in this: for example, how could anyone record the events of creation when there have been no eyewitnesses? In later Judaism, as also in Christianity, it became normal to say that these details had been supernaturally revealed to Moses, the supposed author of the Pentateuch. But no one doubted that everything happened just as it was written.

EMBEDDING

Second, we have the phenomenon I refer to as 'embedding'. By this I mean that within narratives there are sometimes passages that really belong to some other genre. The most striking example is the way the narrative of the Pentateuch contains a lengthy section of legislation within itself. Although the Pentateuch is overall a narrative, there is an enormous set of laws, setting out in great detail how the people of Israel are to live as a society and especially how they are to regulate their ritual behaviour. The laws are integrated into the narrative by the fiction that they were all revealed to Moses on Mount Sinai, but it is pretty clear that they must have originally had an independent existence in which they formed a freestanding legislative code. The phenomenon can be seen in miniature in the case of the Ten Commandments, which enunciate a number of principles of conduct widely observed both in Israel and in other cultures, yet which are said to have been spoken by Moses on a particular occasion, and which begin with a short historical preamble identifying the God who issues these commands as the one who had recently brought the Israelites out of Egypt (Exodus 20:1–17; also Deuteronomy 5:1–21). We shall look at law in the Hebrew Bible in its own right below, but here simply note that the laws are all embedded in narrative: there is no 'law book' in the Bible, only narrative containing law.

Other examples of embedding can be seen where the historical books contain poems. In 2 Samuel 1:19–27 there is a fine lament by David over the death of Saul and Jonathan in battle against the Philistines, which is actually said within the text itself to have been quoted from a book called 'the book of Jashar', which presumably was a compendium of songs or poems. This lament makes excellent sense in its narrative context, but the same cannot be said of all embedded poems. The Song of Hannah, for example (1 Samuel 2:1–10), relates rather loosely to its context, speaking indeed of the way God has granted a child to someone who had been reckoned 'barren', yet also praising him as the God who overcomes the mighty and exalts the poor, which is not so relevant to Hannah's immediate situation. Similar things can be said of the psalm embedded in the short story of Jonah (Jonah 2:2–9), which is supposed to be a prayer Jonah uttered while inside the great fish, but which refers to him entering the temple after being nearly drowned but does not mention the fish at all. The two great poems traditionally called the Benedictus and the Magnificat in Luke's Gospel (respectively Luke 1:68–79 and 1:46–55) are similarly embedded in narrative and also do not quite fit: the Magnificat, clearly modelled on the Song of Hannah, again refers to God overcoming the mighty, while the Benedictus speaks of the child it celebrates as born of the house of David, which does not fit John the Baptist, to whose father it is attributed, but would make more sense as an early Christian poem about Jesus. Some people think Paul's Letters also contain some embedded hymns—the major candidate is Philippians 2:6–11—but this is more controversial.

THE PURPOSE OF NARRATIVES

Third, we should ask what was the purpose of recording all this narrative. The existence of royal annals shows that ancient Israelites were interested in preserving a record of certain past events, just as were other people of the ancient Near East. But the narrative in the Hebrew Bible goes well beyond the annalistic. In the case of 2 Samuel, for example, it preserves an account of the great king David that is far from flattering, and that no king would have wanted in his annals: an account of his adultery and murder, his schemings and his sad old age. It is easier to believe that some of this material was written with the entertainment of an audience in mind, and this is even clearer if one thinks, with minimalists, that it is mostly fiction. But entertainment alone will not account for the enormously long extent of the whole Deuteronomistic History, which contains so many different kinds of narrative. Any explanation of the reasons for compiling such a work must be hypothetical, but one important suggestion is that the History was a vehicle for Israel to acknowledge the guilt of its past actions and so look to the future for divine mercy and forgiveness. Though the work itself says little about a possible resurgence of the nation after the disaster of exile, its very existence may be the result of a desire to confess the wrongdoing of the past and thereby to persuade God to relent and allow a new beginning.

These observations about Hebrew narrative may have some bearing on the interpretation of Acts in the New Testament. It is formally introduced as the second volume of Luke's Gospel:

In the first book, O Theophilus, I have dealt with all that Jesus began to do and teach, until the day when he was taken up, after he had given commandment through the Holy Spirit to the apostles whom he had chosen.

(Acts 1:1–2)

But it is not much like a Gospel, and scholars debate what genre in the Graeco-Roman world it most resembles. It is curious that the second half of the book claims to rest on eye-witness testimony, through a number of passages written in the first person plural (the 'we' passages), whereas the first half is written, like the Gospels, in the third person. Acts seems to have two clear aims, beyond merely chronicling the deeds of the apostles and especially of Paul. One is to show that the strains and tensions between Paul and the other apostles, which are clear in Paul's letters, were comparatively minor and easily resolved. The other is to present Christianity as posing no threat to the good order of the Roman Empire, which never had any quarrel with Paul or indeed any other apostle: opposition came from Jewish groups and rulers, never from the Roman authorities, who respected Paul in particular as a Roman citizen. The Christian faith thus emerges as non-subversive and also as internally consistent and 'catholic'—that is, agreed by all. Modern scholarship has thrown both these beliefs into doubt, but the author of Acts has certainly done a thorough job in making them appear plausible. Acts thus has an apologetic aim, attempting to smooth the path of the Christian community throughout the Empire. The author must have intended it to be read by non-Christians, even if those were interested in the Christian movement.

PROPHECY AND APOCALYPTIC

Although narrative books in the Bible are somewhat strange to us, we do have plenty of experience of narrative, whether in history-writing, in novels and short stories, or even in journalism. With prophecy and apocalyptic the territory is much more unfamiliar. Most of the cultures of the ancient Near East had prophets, people believed to be inspired by the gods to bring messages to human beings and especially to kings and rulers, enabling them to know what the future held and so to plan appropriately when contemplating war or other political action. Ancient Israel was no exception, though it was unusual in that its prophets also had the function of interceding with God—carrying messages into the divine realm from the human one and not only the reverse. But what is really unusual is that the 'oracles', as prophetic utterances are known, were recorded in large collections and attributed to specific named prophets. The Hebrew Bible contains the recorded oracles of many prophets, some within the Deuteronomistic History, but most in books attributed to the prophets by name. For the most part these books are extremely complicated, often arranged by theme rather than chronologically and sometimes even on a 'catchword' principle according to which oracles are put together if they happen to contain the same word or proper name. This makes them difficult to read intelligibly, and a lot of reconstruction has to be done to establish whether any given oracle is really likely to derive from the prophet it is attributed to, and to discover a probable historical setting in which it might have been delivered. Because our knowledge of the detail of Israel's history is so sketchy, precision in ascribing oracles to likely historical backgrounds is often impossible.

PROPHECIES OF DOOM

In general it can be said that earlier prophets, such as Amos and Isaiah, who worked in the eighth century, were concerned with prophesying disaster to the two Hebrew kingdoms. In that period the Assyrians, based in what is now Iraq, first became a serious threat to the nations of Syria–Palestine, and both Amos and Isaiah believed that the fate of the kingdoms depended very much on what decisions the Assyrians might make about expanding their empire westwards. Whether either prophet thought that beyond disaster there would be any kind of restoration of Israel remains unclear, but it is fairly certain that they foretold defeat by Assyria in the short term:

> Hear this word which I take up over you in lamentation,
> O house of Israel:
> 'Fallen, no more to rise,
> is the virgin Israel;
> forsaken on her land,
> with none to raise her up.'

> For thus says the LORD God:
> 'The city that went forth a thousand

> shall have a hundred left,
> and that which went forth a hundred
> shall have ten left
> to the house of Israel.'

(Amos 5:1–3)

The same theme of coming doom engaged the minds of Jeremiah and Ezekiel, who prophesied in the sixth century, when the threat to the kingdom of Judah came from the Babylonians, who had conquered and taken over the Assyrian Empire. But both of them lived through the conquest of Judah and began to think that on the other side of this disaster the God of Israel would bring about a restoration: Ezekiel even went into some detail about the form it would take, with the Judaeans who had been taken off into exile in Babylonia restored to their own land, and the ruined temple rebuilt and reconsecrated. But the most optimistic of all the prophets was the writer known as Deutero-Isaiah, the author of Isaiah 40–55, who believed that divine wrath was now irrevocably past, and that Israel had only good to expect from the future. There was indeed a return from exile, much less glorious than he had expected, but enough to ensure that his words of hope were remembered and copied. The rebuilding of the temple did indeed occur, urged on by the prophets Haggai and Zechariah. Words of doom were no longer the norm for prophets, who started to utter oracles of hope and blessing and to promise good things for the future.

HOPEFUL PROPHECY

Late on in the post-exilic period, during the Persian or Hellenistic ages, prophecy started to take a somewhat new twist. Direct prediction in literal terms began to give way to cryptic messages, often using allegorical images to stand for world powers. We see this particularly in the book of Daniel, written in the second century BC. Christians and Jews alike treated Daniel as prophecy, and in the Christian Bible it is reckoned as the fourth of the Major Prophets, along with Isaiah, Jeremiah, and Ezekiel. But in later Judaism it came to be classed as one of the Writings rather than among the Prophets, and this may reflect an evaluation of it as atypical of the prophets. Short, pithy oracles are replaced with lengthy and involved allegories, and the message seems to be directed to a small in-group of faithful believers rather than to the nation as a whole. The difference is often signalled by calling Daniel 'apocalyptic' rather than prophecy. In modern usage the word generally conveys a sense of universal destruction ('Apocalypse Now'), but in biblical studies this is not necessarily the case: what Daniel foretells does concern the whole political world-order, but the book is not about any sort of cosmic cataclysm, something that is in fact extremely rare in the Hebrew Bible. But it has a cryptic character unlike that of most prophecy.

The New Testament contains one apocalyptic work, as measured by these criteria, though it calls itself a book of prophecy: the book of Revelation. This work probably comes from late in the first century, and it shows how Christians had internalized Jewish prophecy and apocalyptic by that time. Indeed, it is from this book that the term apocalypse derives, since in Greek it is called the Apocalypse of John (*apokalupsis ioannou*). Revelation consists of what seems to be a series of visions of the end-time, probably to be read as alternative versions of these events rather than as linear in character. Though it hardly ever quotes explicitly from the Hebrew Bible, it draws on biblical imagery, and in many ways the visions resemble those of Ezekiel and Zechariah. Its overall theme is the coming overthrow of the Roman Empire, described as 'Babylon'. Notoriously, Christians down the ages have updated the reference, making Babylon mean whatever human power they have been opposed to: at the Reformation Protestants took it to signify the papacy, and in the twentieth century many Americans interpreted it as the Soviet Union. Because apocalyptic is cryptic, it is always open to this kind of reinterpretation. The prophetic books of the Hebrew Bible have also often been interpreted in creative ways and made to refer to whatever crisis people in any given time have found themselves in. But it seems clear that both prophecy and apocalyptic originally had a specific reference in mind, anchored in the period of writing.

LAW

Like other nations, ancient Israel had various laws to order society. As we saw above, these laws do not occur in a 'raw' state in the

Hebrew Bible, but only embedded in the story of Moses in the books of the Pentateuch. All of them are attributed to God as lawgiver, and are supposed to have been mediated through the mouth of Moses. Most strikingly, the entire book of Deuteronomy is cast in the form of a monologue by Moses at the point where the Israelites are about to enter the Promised Land. The other laws, in Exodus, Leviticus, and Numbers, are supposed to have been given to him on Mount Sinai during the period when the Israelite tribes were wandering in the desert between Egypt and Palestine.

A COMMON LEGAL INHERITANCE

But on close examination it is clear that most if not all the laws in fact reflect conditions within the land of Israel. This is true even of the Ten Commandments, where, for example, people are not to envy each other their houses or their domestic animals—neither of these a possibility in the desert. The laws in the Hebrew Bible are essentially similar to many other laws known from the ancient Near East, most obviously the famous *Code of Hammurabi*, drafted in Mesopotamia in the second millennium BC and widely known across the whole Middle East—it exists in many copies. There are often points of contact between Israelite and Mesopotamian laws, so close that the only satisfactory hypothesis is that the Israelites were familiar with the Mesopotamian legal tradition. The most famous example is the 'law of the goring ox':

> When an ox gores a man or a woman to death, the ox shall be stoned, and its flesh shall not be eaten; but the owner of the ox shall not be liable. If the ox has been accustomed to gore in the past, and its owner has been warned but has not restrained it, and it kills a man or a woman, the ox shall be stoned, and its owner also shall be put to death.
>
> (Exodus 21:28–29)

> If an ox, when it was walking along the street, gored a nobleman to death, that case is not subject to claim. If a nobleman's ox was a gorer and his city council had made it known to him that it was a gorer, but he did not pad its horns or tie up his ox, and that ox gored to death a member of the aristocracy, he shall give one half mina of silver.
>
> (*Code of Hammurabi* 250–51)

DISTINCTIVENESS OF ISRAELITE LAW

Nevertheless, Israel's law codes do have certain features that make them rather distinctive. The first is the attribution to God. The *Code of Hammurabi* is attributed to the king of that name, though it is said that he was raised up to be a lawgiver by the great gods. Israelite law however is never attributed to Moses in that way; Moses is only a mouthpiece for God. Second, Israelite law concerns itself not only with civil regulation but also with the details of worship and sacrifice. Other nations had rules about such things, but they did not appear in their national law codes—they were the kind of thing priests knew about, not the populace at large. And thirdly, some of the most important Israelite laws are couched in the second person—'you shall/shall not do X', while others are in the standard ancient Near Eastern form 'if someone does X, then the penalty is Y'. This so-called 'apodeictic' or absolute law, by contrast with the standard 'casuistic' form, occurs occasionally in the laws of other nations, but in Israel it is developed to a much greater extent: the whole of the Ten Commandments, for example, is apodeictic in form. A possible explanation of all three features is that in Israel the laws were in the custodianship of priests, who had the task of making sure that they were known, rather than of secular officials, judges or civil servants. We know from the book of Haggai that it was the priests who gave rulings on matters of legal dispute (Haggai 2:10–14), and they also seem to have acted as a court of appeal in hard cases (Exodus 22:8). A priestly provenance for much Israelite law would certainly go some way to explaining the mass of ceremonial regulation which fills so much of Exodus, Leviticus, and Numbers.

If we leave aside the detailed regulations concerned with worship and with ritual purity, we are left with three basic codes in the Hebrew Bible that seem likely to have existed in an independent form before they were incorporated into the Pentateuch and ascribed to God's revelation through Moses. These are the so-called Covenant Code (Exodus 21–24), the Holiness Code (Leviticus 17–26), and the Code of Deuteronomy (Deuteronomy 12–26). Of these, the Covenant Code seems likely to be the earliest; it may go back before the time when Israel had a king, that is, into the tenth or eleventh century BC. It consists mainly of 'civil' laws about the ordering of society, prohibiting murder, theft, and corrupt legal practice. Even at this stage it includes basic provision for regular worship at local sanctuaries ('high places'), though there is none of the detailed regulation of the sacrificial system that we find so plentifully in Leviticus.

HISTORY OF THE LAW CODES

Whenever it is possible to compare the Covenant Code with the laws in Deuteronomy, the latter seems to be derivative from the former or to represent an updated version. This is clearest in the laws about slaves:

> When you buy a Hebrew slave, he shall serve six years, and in the seventh he shall go out free, for nothing. If he comes in single, he shall go out single; if he comes in married, then his wife shall go out with him. If his master gives him a wife and she bears him sons or daughters, the wife and her children shall be her master's and he shall go out alone.
>
> (Exodus 21:2–4)

> If your brother, a Hebrew man or a Hebrew woman, is sold to you, he shall serve you six years, and in the seventh year you shall let him go free from you. And when you let him go free from you, you shall not let him go empty-handed; you shall furnish him liberally out of your flock, out of your threshing floor, and out of your wine press ... And to your bondwoman you shall do likewise.
>
> (Deuteronomy 15:12–14, 17)

The normal hypothesis is that Deuteronomy is a reworking of the laws in Exodus at a later time, probably well into the monarchy and perhaps not long before its demise in the sixth century. Biblical scholarship has tended to associate Deuteronomy with the reformist movement promulgated by King Josiah in the 620s or so. This is because, in sharp contrast with Exodus, Deuteronomy does not allow sacrificial worship at local sanctuaries but insists that it is to take place only at the 'place which the LORD your God will choose' (Deuteronomy 12:5), generally thought to be a coded way of referring to Jerusalem. Josiah did indeed try to centralize worship at the Jerusalem temple (2 Kings 23), and much of Deuteronomy would make good sense if it came from his court.

The Holiness Code (sometimes called H) is part of the Priestly strand in the Pentateuch, which probably puts it in the early post-exilic period, though it may rest on an underlying code which is older. Though, again, it does have some rules about ritual, it also contains a lot of social legislation, including the commands to 'love your neighbour as yourself' (Leviticus 19:18) and, perhaps even more surprisingly to 'love the resident alien as yourself' (19:34). These provisions again make us wonder how far the material in these codes is exactly what we should call 'law'. Some of them, just like the ethical injunctions in Paul's letters, are not really enforceable legislation, but moral *teaching*. If it is indeed to priests that we owe much of the law in the Pentateuch, then their role was probably not so much a judicial as a didactic one, or rather it must have combined both functions. The Hebrew word usually translated 'law', *torah*, certainly came in later times to mean teaching or instruction rather than simply legislation, and when Jews today speak of the Pentateuch as *torah* they are thinking of it as a guide for living, not as law in the narrow sense of enforceable regulations. Too great an attention to parallels with ancient Near Eastern law codes can be slightly misleading. We do not possess anything from ancient Israel that is truly parallel to the great ancient Near Eastern codes, in spite of the similarities in detailed content noted above.

By the age of the New Testament, *torah* had come to cover much more than simply the Pentateuchal legislation, embracing the so-called 'oral law' as well as what stands written in the Hebrew Bible. The oral law is the tradition of scribal, priestly, and eventually rabbinic reflection on the regulations in the Hebrew Bible, producing over time a complete ethical and ritual system by which to live, and in due course coming to include the 613 commandments incumbent on Orthodox Jews. No such system was yet in force at the time when the Hebrew Bible was being compiled, but its beginnings can be seen there.

PSALMODY

A lot of the Hebrew Bible is in verse rather than prose, as can be seen from any modern translation. Many prophetic oracles, already discussed, are expressed in verse; but in this section we are concerned with perhaps the most important verse compositions in the Hebrew

Bible, the book of Psalms. The origins of the biblical Psalms are shrouded in mystery. Commentators in the nineteenth and early twentieth century thought they were all post-exilic, and Julius Wellhausen (1844–1918, one of the most important nineteenth-century Old Testament scholars) described the Psalter as the 'hymn-book of the Second Temple'. Later in the twentieth century, especially under the influence of the Norwegian scholar Sigmund Mowinckel (1884–1965), it became normal to think of many of them as going back to the early years of the monarchy—even in some cases to David himself, to whom the whole collection is traditionally attributed.

ORIGINS OF THE PSALMS

At the moment most scholarly attention is fixed on the final collection and ordering of the book of Psalms, which just about everyone thinks happened in the post-exilic age, and many have lost interest in the question of the origins of the individual psalms. What can be said, though, is that (as with law) there are significant parallels with other ancient Near Eastern cultures, and especially with the texts from Ugarit (Ras Shamra) in Syria, dating from the late second millennium BC, that are thought by many to be the closest literary texts to much of the Hebrew Bible. This parallel means that some of the biblical Psalms *could* be very old, though it does not prove that they are: literary forms are very tenacious across time. Perhaps the closest parallel to Ugaritic poetry can be found in the structure of Psalm 29, with its 'step' arrangement:

> The voice of the LORD is upon the waters:
>   the God of glory thunders,
>   the LORD, upon many waters.
>   The voice of the LORD is powerful,
>   the voice of the LORD is full of majesty.
>   The voice of the LORD shakes the wilderness,
>   the LORD shakes the wilderness of Kadesh.
>
> (Psalm 29:3–4, 8)

The Psalms that Mowinckel claimed for the Jerusalem temple in the days of the early monarchy were mostly those that celebrate the kingship of the God of Israel (93, 96–99). He thought that there was some kind

of Enthronement Festival in Judah, in which either God was symboli-
cally re-enthroned each year, or the king was enthroned as his
representative. The Hebrew Bible does not tell us that any such festival existed, but it is plausible enough: other cultures in the Middle
East had a New Year celebration in which something like this
happened, known in Babylonia as the *akitu* festival. Such a festival
would also be a plausible context for the recitation of the creation
narratives in Genesis, since it was at the *akitu* festival that the creation epic of Mesopotamia, *Enuma elish*, was ceremonially recited.

But the majority of Psalms would not belong in any particular festival, since they are all-purpose texts. Hermann Gunkel (1862–1932),
Mowinckel's teacher, had divided them into various classes or types:
communal laments, individual laments, communal thanksgivings,
individual thanksgivings, and so on. As a matter of fact it is quite
difficult to distinguish the prayers of individuals from those of the
group, since it is not uncommon for the individual 'I' to stand for a
large group—compare the personification of the desolate city of
Jerusalem as a single man in Lamentations 3—while it is perfectly
possible for an individual worshipper to use a corporate Psalm to
express his or her own feelings, as is clear from the use by individuals
nowadays of hymns written to be sung by a congregation. What
complicates the matter further is that in ancient cultures worshippers
often did not recite psalms themselves, but employed experts to do
it on their behalf. We are not to think of ancient Israelite worship
as involving a congregation all standing to sing hymns together, on
a Protestant model, but as something more like the worship in
Eastern Orthodox churches, or in Catholic churches before the
Second Vatican Council, with priests attending to their part in the
liturgy while individual lay worshippers get on with theirs.

TORAH PSALMS

Among the later Psalms are some that reflect the growth of the
torah system just described: one may think especially of the longest
Psalm in the Psalter, Psalm 119, which is an acrostic psalm. Each of
its 22 sections is devoted to one letter of the Hebrew alphabet, with
each of the eight verses in each section beginning with the same
letter. It is a hymn in praise of the *torah*, of which various synonyms
occur again and again, rather like ringing the changes on church

bells. Also notable is Psalm 19, which combines praise for the sun as one of God's greatest creations with a second part in which the brightness of the sun is compared with that of the *torah*:

> The heavens are telling the glory of God;
> and the firmament proclaims his handiwork.
> Day to day pours forth speech,
> and night to night declares knowledge.
> There is no speech, nor are there words;
> their voice is not heard;
> yet their voice goes out through all the earth,
> and their words to the end of the world.
> In them he has set a tent for the sun,
> which comes forth like a bridegroom leaving his chamber,
> and like a strong man runs its course with joy.
> Its rising is from the end of the heavens,
> and its circuit to the end of them;
> and there is nothing hid from its heat.
> The law of the LORD is perfect,
> reviving the soul;
> the testimony of the LORD is sure,
> making wise the simple;
> the precepts of the LORD are right,
> rejoicing the heart;
> the commandment of the LORD is pure,
> enlightening the eyes;
> the fear of the LORD is clean,
> enduring for ever;
> the ordinances of the LORD are true,
> and righteous altogether.
> More to be desired are they than gold,
> even much fine gold;
> sweeter also than honey
> and drippings of the honeycomb.

(Psalm 19:2–11)

Taken as a finished whole the Psalter probably does meet Wellhausen's description of it as 'the hymn-book of the Second Temple'. Even so, it is noteworthy that in the service of the synagogue as it comes down to us from the first few centuries AD there is no comprehensive use of the Psalms, only of a certain selection. Only in Christian monasticism did there develop a use of the whole book of Psalms, often sung in numerical order except for a few that had come to be specially associated with morning or evening. Rabbinic Judaism did not on the whole treat the book of Psalms as a collection for worship but as a book for study, like all the other books of the Hebrew Bible.

WISDOM

The other great collection of material in verse is represented by the wisdom books, Proverbs, Ecclesiastes (Qoheleth), the Song of Solomon, and Job in the Hebrew canon, and Sirach (Ecclesiasticus) and the Wisdom of Solomon among the deuterocanonical/apocryphal books. Wisdom books, like law and psalmody, are closely paralleled in other ancient Near Eastern cultures, where from very remote times there were collections of proverbs and wise sayings like those in Proverbs, and also semi-dramatic dialogues and reflections on the meaning of life, somewhat akin to Job. The main parallels for the Song of Solomon (or Song of Songs) are to be found in Egypt, where erotic poetry has a long history. The biblical wisdom literature is interesting theologically, because it seems to oscillate between a quite secular attitude and an insistence on 'the fear of the LORD', that is, proper reverence and respect for God, as the foundation of true wisdom. One cannot isolate separate strata containing these two different attitudes; rather they intermingle in every chapter of a book such as Proverbs.

ORIGINS OF WISDOM

Many of the proverbs must go back to folk wisdom, but in the ancient Near East the collection of them into compendia was the work of court scribes, and it is interesting that alongside sayings belonging to everyday village life we find proverbs that presuppose life at court:

> When you sit down to eat with a ruler, observe carefully what is before you, and put a knife to your throat if you are a man given to appetite. Do not desire his delicacies, for they are deceptive food.
>
> (Proverbs 23:1–3)

Many proverbs are about the king. How sophisticated the genre could be can be seen from Proverbs 30:

> Three things are stately in their tread;
> four are stately in their stride:
> the lion, which is mightiest among beasts
> and does not turn back before any;
> the strutting cock, the he-goat,
> and a king striding before his people.
>
> (Proverbs 30:29–31)

In Job and Ecclesiastes, both works from the post-exilic age (Ecclesiastes may be from as late as the third century BC), the tradition of wise reflection on life turns in on itself and becomes sharply self-critical and sceptical. The ancient world affords few parallels to these works until the writings of the Greek Sceptics. Whereas in older wisdom, as represented in Proverbs, it is assumed that anyone who applies his or her mind to analysing the world and human life in it will become 'wise'—an assumption that re-emerges in Sirach—Job and Ecclesiastes put forward the radical idea that real wisdom, in the sense of a comprehensive knowledge and understanding of the world, is unattainable. Job 28 argues that human beings have shown great ingenuity in mining gold and silver and precious stones, and in all manner of engineering works, but they cannot find the way to wisdom, which lies beyond human capabilities. In Ecclesiastes consideration of the physical world reveals that everything repeats itself on an endless cycle, and there is, as a modern person would put it, no 'point' in any human activity, since everything we do leads only to death. In Job a similarly sceptical conclusion follows from analysing the state of an innocent man who is afflicted with illness and personal disaster, and showing that (contrary to what his 'friends' tell him) he is not to blame for them, and hence the age-old assumption that suffering is caused by sin will not hold water.

THE SONG OF SOLOMON

The Song of Songs (or Solomon) is an extraordinary work to find in the Hebrew Bible, and its presence has caused much embarrassment because of its erotic content. It is certainly a fine example of Hebrew poetry, and both Jews and Christians from very ancient times have read it allegorically, of the relation between Israel or the individual believer and God. It should be noted that by the time the Song was written (perhaps in the second century BC) there was an extensive body of Jewish mystical writing, of which there are many examples among the Dead Sea Scrolls, and the Song could therefore have been written with allegorical intent in the first place. If it is seen as secular love poetry (and it nowhere mentions God), then our ideas of wisdom literature will have to expand to include such works, of which there is no other example in the Hebrew Bible.

WISDOM INFLUENCE

Wisdom as an intellectual and social movement clearly had an influence beyond the learned scribes who wrote and transmitted wisdom books. The prophets often betray an awareness of wisdom teaching, and some have suggested that Isaiah in particular was a scribe or royal adviser at the court of King Hezekiah, which might explain his ease of access to the king as well as his use of proverbial expressions. Wisdom literature is the nearest Hebrew (or ancient Near Eastern) culture came to what in Greece would become philosophy: ordered, rational thinking about the meaning of life and the constitution of the world, driven by the human intellect rather than by any assumption of divine revelation. Early Greek culture had it too: an example is Hesiod's *Works and Days*.

THE PERSONIFICATION OF WISDOM AND TORAH

Sirach shows that wisdom continued to flourish down into the second century BC, retaining many of the assumptions about the intelligibility of the world that we find in Proverbs, and rejecting the sceptical counter-blast from Job and Ecclesiastes. In Sirach, however, wisdom is wedded to *torah*: there is no longer any distinction between what the law teaches and what the sages advise, but *torah* is the true wisdom (and hence eminently accessible, against what Job had argued). The equation of wisdom and law, which we find in Sirach 24:23 ('all this [i.e. wisdom] is the book of the covenant of the Most High God, the law which Moses

commanded us as an inheritance for the congregations of Jacob'),
depends on another development that had gained strength over the
years: the personification of wisdom as a kind of goddess (the
Hebrew word for wisdom, *hokhmah*, is feminine), who acts as an
intermediary between God and the creation. There is no agreement
on how and why this development occurred. Some think it was to
provide worshippers of the male, lone God of Israel with some of
the advantages of a feminine element in the divine realm. It may
also represent a tendency in many religions to personify virtues and
human qualities as having their origin among the gods. The personification is already quite advanced in the book of Proverbs, in
passages perhaps deriving from quite soon after the exile:

> The LORD created me [wisdom] at the beginning of his work
> the first of his acts of old.
> Ages ago I was set up,
> at the first, before the beginning of the earth.
> When he established the heavens I was there,
> when he drew a circle on the face of the deep,
> when he made firm the skies above,
> when he established the foundations of the deep.
> Then I was beside him, like a master workman;
> and I was daily his delight.
>
> (Proverbs 8:22–23, 27–28, 30)

It is this personified wisdom that Sirach identifies with the *torah*. It
is also the subject of a lengthy treatment in the book known as the
Wisdom of Solomon, which derives from the first century BC. In
both works it is clear that wisdom is a kind of divine person, and it
is no surprise that such passages were pressed into service by early
Christians seeking scriptural warrant for the doctrine of the Trinity.
The personification of wisdom does not seem to have called in
question the basic monotheism of the Jewish religion: wisdom is
clearly subordinate to God wherever it is mentioned. But it is a
reminder that Jewish monotheism is sophisticated and subtle, and
allows for more than simply a kind of monad in the divine realm.
In a way the proliferation of angels in later books of the Hebrew
Bible and Apocrypha, and in the New Testament, is a similar
example. There is no question of these beings acting as rivals to the

one God, yet they do to some extent bridge the gulf between the supreme Being and the human world.

GOSPELS

What is a Gospel? At one level everyone knows what it is: an account of the life, teaching, miracles, death, and resurrection of Jesus. In this the Gospels seem to be rather like the narrative books of the Hebrew Bible—Kings, for example. But closer inspection raises some questions, and five will concern us here.

INSIDERS OR OUTSIDERS?

First, are the Gospels written for those inside the church, to edify and instruct them, or are they evangelistic, aimed at people outside the church, to convert them? This can be put in the technical terms of New Testament scholarship by asking whether they are *didache* (teaching) or *kerygma* (proclamation). The beginning of Luke poses this question quite sharply, where the writer says that the book is intended for 'Theophilus' (we don't know whether this is a real person or any 'God-lover', which is the meaning of the Greek name) to instruct him in the matters on which he has already been partially informed (or misinformed). Does this mean that Luke was written to convince a partly-informed non-Christian of the truth of the Christian message, or does it mean that it was written for someone who was already a Christian but who needed more information about Jesus than he had so far acquired? There is no agreement on this. There are features in the Gospels that point in both directions. Matthew's Sermon on the Mount (5–8) looks like teaching, laying down the rules for those inside the community of the church. But much of Mark's terser account strikes many readers as intended to be read by non-Christians, to bring about their conversion. In practice all the Gospels have historically functioned in both ways, but saying what was the original intention is far from easy.

HISTORY OR PROPAGANDA?

Second, should the Gospels be seen as a form of historiography (even if not everything in them is factually true) or as a form of fiction, perhaps (on the 'kerygmatic' interpretation) propaganda for the Christian movement? We have already faced a similar issue in the case of the narrative books of the Hebrew Bible, and have noted that there the modern distinction between fact and fiction may not always be appropriate: we may be able to decide whether an alleged incident is or is not likely to have taken place as described, but the writers had not formulated this distinction in their own minds. The Gospels are probably the distillation of a couple of generations of oral transmission of the story of Jesus, and by the time it came to be written down, people no longer knew what was fact and what fiction. Modern New Testament scholars have developed criteria for trying to decide (see chapter 6), but such criteria were not used by the Gospel writers or compilers themselves: everything was transmitted as though it were equally historically accurate, even though the presence of parallel versions of the same story with differences in detail shows that this cannot be so in fact. However, Luke's Prologue is important again here, because it states that he had read a number of different versions of the story of Jesus and had established a true version himself—showing that he at least had our awareness of the fact/fiction distinction, even if we cannot therefore necessarily trust his critical judgement on any given event or saying. The Gospels certainly appear to claim that they are historiography, which means that there are several ancient genres they clearly do not belong to—for example, myth or fable. John, which is treated with most suspicion by modern readers because it seems to be all interpretation of Jesus with very little fact, is arguably the Gospel that makes the strongest factual claim: 'This is the disciple who is bearing witness to these things, and who has written these things; and we know that his testimony is true' (John 21:24).

INTERRELATIONSHIP OF THE GOSPELS

Third, how are the four Gospels interrelated? Readers often assume that they are four separate eyewitness accounts of the life of Jesus, which therefore corroborate each other even though they differ on points of detail. But a closer reading shows that Matthew, Mark, and Luke (the 'Synoptic' Gospels) tell a very similar story, while John's account overlaps very little until the passion story, and even there has really significant differences. The similarities among the Synoptics are often verbal, with whole phrases and sentences being almost identical between two or all three of the accounts. This has led most New Testament scholars to believe that there is actual literary continuity among the Synoptics. If we adopt the common modern belief that Mark is the oldest Gospel, then it seems that both Matthew and Luke drew upon it, because often they tell the same story as Mark in very similar words. (This is what the Prologue to Luke might lead us to expect anyway, if Mark is one of the versions of the life of Jesus he was familiar with.) The simplest solution of the 'Synoptic Problem', as it is known, is that Matthew used Mark, and Luke used both Mark and Matthew, or alternatively that Luke used Mark, and Matthew used both Mark and Luke. But for a number of reasons these simple scenarios do not satisfy most scholars. There is indeed material not in Mark that is shared by Matthew and Luke, but there are problems in thinking that either of them got this material by reading the other. The shared non-Marcan material always seems to occur at a different place in the story in Matthew and in Luke. And sometimes one of the writers seems to have preserved what looks like its original form, and sometimes the other! This has led most (though by no means all) scholars to believe that as well as Mark, Matthew and Luke had another source for their Gospels, the source Q referred to in chapter 2 above. In addition there are stories and sayings found only in Matthew or only in Luke, and these are usually called M and L: they may never have existed as independent writings, and we do not know how the Gospel-writers came by them.

A lot of effort has gone into reconstructing the hypothetical Q, and there are even commentaries on it. One of the most striking features is that it seems to have consisted only of sayings of Jesus, not of stories about miracles or other events, and not to have included a narrative about Jesus' trial and crucifixion. This reminds us that the Gospels we have are not the only kind of Christian document that could have developed. Strikingly similar to Q, as already noted, is the work known as the *Gospel of Thomas*. This shows that a 'Gospel' containing only teaching was felt by some in the early church to be adequate as a foundation document for the Christian community. They did not share our assumption that a Gospel 'must' contain narrative as well as teaching. Some may have seen Jesus principally as a great teacher, as many non-Christians do today, and have been rather uninterested in what he did or in what happened to him.

The relation of the Synoptics to John has also long been a disputed question. The story is recognizably about the same person, who taught, worked miracles (John calls them 'signs'), was tried and executed and rose again from the dead. Yet there is scarcely any overlap in the stories of Jesus: apart from the feeding of the five thousand, there are no miracles in John that also occur in the Synoptics, and Jesus' teaching has a radically different tone. Where the sayings in the Synoptics tend to be short and pithy, in John they consist of lengthy discourses, the subject matter of which tends to be Jesus himself and his identity as the Son or God, where the Synoptic sayings are mostly about human behaviour and lifestyle. There are no parables in John. The difference is obvious from the first chapter of John, which is a long discourse on the divine status of Jesus as the Word of God rather than a nativity story as in Matthew and Luke. Even if there is some use of Synoptic material in John, most of the Gospel must derive from other sources. Whether these sources preserved any historical truth, or whether they are a semi-mythical version of the life of Jesus, is widely disputed.

LOCAL OR UNIVERSAL GOSPELS?

Fourth, was each Gospel written for a specific Christian community, or are they intended for all Christians? In recent years, as we have seen, there has been a tendency to see them as community-specific. If this is true, then one can work out from each Gospel what were some of the cutting-edge questions for its particular community: in Matthew's church, for example, there were big questions about the continuing validity of the *torah*—hence all the material in which Jesus seems to position himself in relation to current Judaism, such as the sayings in the Sermon on the Mount about obedience to the teaching of Moses. If this general hypothesis is correct, then Christianity was a highly diverse movement by the early second century, and in particular the 'Johannine community' was wildly different from the 'Marcan community', representing a Christian approach with a much more mystical bent and preaching a Christ who was a heavenly redeemer rather than the rather down-to-earth figure of Mark and the other Synoptics. But by no means all New Testament scholars believe that the hypothesis is correct. Luke's Prologue, again, suggests that he at least looked around the churches of his day to find his information and that his clear purpose was to *replace* the already existing Gospels. The same seems likely in respect to Matthew and Mark: Matthew reads like a *correction* of Mark, not as an alternative version intended to stand alongside it. As things worked out in the church, by the mid-second century Christians had come to accept the four Gospels as somehow complementing each other— leading to great problems over how to reconcile the accounts; but in the age when the Gospels were being written each seems to have been designed to *supersede* its predecessors. Even after the church accepted a four-Gospel canon, there were attempts to produce 'harmonies' of the four, fitting all the events in all of them into a consistent narrative. The classic attempt to do this is the *Diatessaron*, by Tatian, which continued to be used in the Syrian church down into the fourth century. Gospel harmonies are still produced today, because the problem of having four partly inconsistent Gospels is still felt in the churches. But probably none of the Gospel-writers originally intended his Gospel to be read alongside others, but rather to replace existing ones with something better.

GENRE OF THE GOSPELS

Fifth, are there any parallels to the Gospels, or are they a genre all of their own? Biblical scholars naturally tend to look to the Hebrew Bible for parallels, but these are few and far between. The stories of Jesus' birth and infancy in the opening chapters of Matthew and Luke do resemble biblical stories such as those of the birth of Samson or Samuel, and in Luke the stories are actually written in a biblical style of Greek, that is, in a style imitated from the LXX and different from the 'modern' (first-century) Greek of the rest of the Gospel. But this only highlights how unbiblical the writing is in the rest of the Gospel. John's narrative is unlike anything in the rest of the Bible in the Old or New Testament. It is often suggested that we should look for parallels in contemporary

Greek writing, rather than in the Hebrew Bible. Recently a strong case has been made for seeing the Gospels as akin to the 'Lives' of heroes and teachers of the Graeco-Roman period, of which a number of examples have come down to us. These probably provide closer parallels to the Gospels than anything in the Old Testament, and it is interesting that they are often strikingly different from each other in style and presentation—so perhaps the diversity among the Gospels, and particularly the differences between John and the Synoptics, ought to be seen as less of a problem than scholars have made it.

THE LETTERS (EPISTLES)

If Graeco-Roman analogies help us to understand the Gospels, this is much more obviously the case where the letters of Paul, and the other New Testament letters, are concerned. The Hebrew Bible has virtually nothing that can be compared with the New Testament letters. Paul clearly began the practice of Christian leaders writing to the communities they had founded, and this is bound up with his own peripatetic style of ministry. Rather than remaining permanently among the new Christians he had evangelized, he went on extensive tours around the eastern Mediterranean, and in between visiting his communities he corresponded with them. His letters are the oldest Christian writings (1 Thessalonians being the very first, as pointed out earlier), and in style they are very similar to the letters of other writers of the time, though they begin and end distinctively with Christian greetings rather than with the greetings then commonplace. But Paul did not write only to communities he had founded, but also (for example in Romans) to those converted by others. He approaches the Roman community respectfully, even awkwardly: 'I long to see you, that I may impart to you some spiritual gift to strengthen you, that is, that we may be mutually encouraged by each other's faith, both your and mine' (Romans 1:11–12). Yet he clearly sees it as his right, because he is Christ's apostle to all the non-Jewish Christians, to give them instruction in the nature of the Christian faith. This is a momentous move, by which Paul establishes the genre of the *encyclical*, a letter to all Christians from an authoritative leader (in later times, of course, the Pope).

THE LETTERS AS SCRIPTURE

This last fact should make us pause before accepting too readily something that is often said about the New Testament writings, that they 'were not written as Scripture'. It is perfectly true that for the earliest Christians only what we now call the Old Testament was 'Scripture'— that is, holy writings received from the past. But the New Testament writings were not intended as ephemeral or casual works. The Gospels all seem to claim a certain authority as the official records of Jesus, with John even designed to look like a Christian replacement for Genesis ('In the beginning ... '). Paul's letters, similarly, address very specific and concrete problems in the individual churches. Yet they are intended to be read and re-read: Clement of Rome, in the early second century, writes to the Corinthian church and reminds them of what Paul had said in 1 Corinthians, taking it for granted that they would have the letter in their hands. Writing a lengthy letter was not a casual act in this period: it was a time-consuming and expensive activity, and people were expected to treasure and guard the document they received, not to throw it away or simply file it when it had been read once. Many classical authors of this period (notably Cicero) published collections of their letters: a letter was a valuable object to be pondered and savoured at leisure, and in the case of Paul's letters, to be read aloud among the Christians assembled for worship. Manuscript evidence suggests that Paul's letters were collected together quite early on, and arranged in their present order: one set of letters to churches, and one of letters to individuals, in each set the order being determined by length.

PSEUDONYMITY

Most scholars agree that not all the letters attributed to Paul are in fact by him. Ephesians is generally seen as a development of themes in Colossians, and Colossians itself is seen by some as pseudo-Paul, though there are many defenders of Pauline authorship. 2 Thessalonians is also widely regarded as spurious. But the major examples of pseudo-Paul are the so-called Pastoral Letters, two to Timothy and one to Titus. In them we find a church which seems to have developed structures and a whole style of integration into the surrounding society that presuppose a later development from that in the churches Paul wrote to. There are orders of ministry, organized societies of widows, and a leadership that has to consider how it will be evaluated by the pagan society around it: this seems a long way removed from Paul. The only way of saving these letters for Paul himself is probably to argue that he was released from prison and had a considerable ministry that continued till late in the first century, so that there was time for considerable changes in the organization of the churches. Most scholars think that the letters were written by disciples and admirers of Paul in his name, but after his time. There remains, as we saw in the last chapter, a question about the legitimacy of writing letters in another person's name, and especially of adopting his persona and inventing circumstantial details about his life: was that really acceptable? The judgement of most that the Pastorals are pseudonymous means that it must have been, however peculiar that seems to us.

There are other letters in the New Testament, by general consent later than those of Paul and generally attributed pseudonymously to other apostolic figures: James, Peter, and John. Like Paul's letters they deal with specific issues in the churches, though James and 1 Peter at least are apparently addressed to a number of different churches (thus also encyclicals), rather than to a single church. The oddity is the 'Epistle to the Hebrews'. This is not in form a letter at all, but something more like a treatise or perhaps a sermon; and, as we have seen, it is not attributed to any specific author. Some people in the early church thought it Pauline, and accordingly placed it next to Romans in their listings, but others did not, and placed it instead with the non-Pauline letters. The great third-century interpreter, Origen, showed clearly that the Greek is different from Paul's. Assigning a definite genre to Hebrews is thus very difficult.

So the Letters are no more uniform generically than the Gospels, and the New Testament, for all that it is so much shorter than the Old, is extremely variegated. Classifying the different works in it is an elusive task.

FURTHER READING

An up-to-date account of Old Testament narrative is provided in David M. Gunn and Danna Nolan Fewell, *Narrative in the Hebrew Bible*, Oxford: Oxford University Press, 1993: this takes in postmodern approaches to the reading of narrative texts. A more traditional source-critical approach can be found in R. G. Kratz, *The Composition of the Narrative Books of the Old Testament*, London: T & T Clark, 2005. On the shorter narrative books an attractive guide is Lawrence M. Wills, *The Jewish Novel in the Ancient World*, Ithaca & London: Cornell University Press, 1995.

A standard history of the prophetic movement in ancient Israel is Joseph Blenkinsopp, *A History of Prophecy in Israel*, Louisville, Ky.: Westminster John Knox, second edition 1996. For the development of apocalyptic a good general guide is John J. Collins, *The Apocalyptic Imagination: An Introduction to Jewish Apocalyptic Literature*, Grand Rapids, Mich.: Eerdmans, 1998, (second edition).

There are not many accessible introductions to Old Testament law, but there is useful material in Joseph Blenkinsopp, *Wisdom and Law in the Old Testament: The Ordering of Law in Israel and Early Judaism*, Oxford: Oxford University Press, 1995.

There are a number of good modern introductions to the Psalms, for example John Day, *The Psalms*, Sheffield: Sheffield Academic Press, 1992, and Susan Gillingham, *The Poems and Psalms of the Hebrew Bible*, Oxford: Oxford University Press, 1994.

The wisdom literature is also well-served: as well as Blenkinsopp's book (see above under law), a classic treatment is James L. Crenshaw, *Old Testament Wisdom: An Introduction*, Louisville, Ky.: Westminster John Knox, 1998 (second edition). More recent, and including some New Testament works, is Katharine J. Dell, *Get Wisdom, Get Insight: An Introduction to Israel's Wisdom Literature*, London: Darton, Longman & Todd, 2000.

The now standard discussion of the genre of the Gospels is Richard Burridge, *What are the Gospels?: A Comparison with Graeco-Roman Biography*, Cambridge: Cambridge University Press, 1992. On the Synoptic Gospels more generally, there is an excellent study-guide: E. P. Sanders and Margaret Davies, *Studying the Synoptic Gospels*, London: SCM, 1989. A survey of the study of John's Gospel is provided by John Ashton, *The Interpretation of John*, Edinburgh: T & T Clark, 1997. On the Gospels in general see J. D. Crossan, *The Birth of Christianity*, Edinburgh: T & T Clark, 1999, and Martin Hengel, *The Four Gospels and the One Gospel of Jesus Christ*, London: SCM, 2000. The chief challenge to the theory of 'local' Gospels is Richard Bauckham, *The Gospels for All Christians: Rethinking the Gospel Audiences*, Edinburgh: T & T Clark, 1998; and for a defence of the eyewitness character of the Gospels, against the general consensus that they are much later than the time of Jesus, see his *Jesus and the Eyewitnesses: The Gospels as Eyewitness Testimony*, Grand Rapids, Mich. and Cambridge: Eerdmans, 2006.

For the New Testament Letters there is a useful essay by Harry Y. Gamble, 'Letters in the New Testament and in the Graeco-Roman World', in John Barton (ed.), *The Biblical World*, vol. 1, London: Routledge, 2002. See also D. E. Aune, *The New Testament in its Literary Environment*, Philadelphia: Westminster, 1987.

4

RELIGIOUS THEMES

The Bible is religious or theological literature. Ancient Israel certainly had writings of a non-religious character, and the early church must have produced 'secular' letters and other documents; but the Bible contains only a selection of the *religious* writings of both. To summarize the themes of the Bible is therefore to engage all the time with theological issues. We begin with the character of God as communicated in the Bible.

THE NATURE OF GOD

A modern theological treatise might begin by asking about the divine nature in itself—what God is like when there's no one else there—before going on to ask how God relates to the world and to human beings upon it. Martin Luther however once remarked that the Bible does not tell us about God so much as about ourselves. At one level this is obviously false: there is a lot about God in the Bible. But at a more profound level it is a wise reminder that we learn of God in the Bible only in relationship with the created order and especially with humankind; and above all in relationship with a chosen people, whether that people is construed as 'Israel' in the Hebrew Bible or as the Christian community, as in the New Testament.

In the Hebrew Bible there are very occasional descriptions of God (most of the time God is hidden from view), such as this, which is found in several places:

> The LORD, the LORD, a God merciful and gracious, slow to anger, and abounding in steadfast love and faithfulness, keeping steadfast love for thousands, forgiving iniquity and transgression and sin, but who will by no means clear the guilty, visiting the iniquity of the fathers upon the children and the children's children, to the third and the fourth generation.
>
> (Exodus 34:6–7; cf. Joel 2:13, Jonah 4:2)

But even here it is God in relation to human beings who is in focus. On the whole this is also true in the New Testament, where the existence and basic nature of God are taken as a given, not discussed, and attention is focused on how the human race relates to that God. When the Letter to the Hebrews lists examples of faith in God, it is God as one who intervenes in human affairs that is the centre of attention: 'whoever would draw near to God must believe that he exists and that he rewards those who seek him' (Hebrews 11:6). It is only in post-biblical streams of thought, in Jewish and Christian mysticism, that we find an interest in the divine nature in itself; and both religions have strains that see such an interest as illegitimate, human beings trying to penetrate into realms into which they have no business to go.

The character of God in both Testaments is thus bound up with the creation of the world and the choice of a special people, and it is only in these two areas that God can be truly known. Both are of equal importance if we are to understand the nature of the biblical God.

GOD AS THE CREATOR OF ALL

The idea that the world owes its origins to a power or powers beyond itself was a commonplace in the ancient Near East, where there were in effect no atheists. In most of the cultures that surrounded Israel there were one or more myths about how the world was brought into being, and in Mesopotamian culture, which exercised the greatest influence on Israel, creation was thought to have arisen as a by-product of a battle among the gods. In the Akkadian epic *Enuma elish* the physical world is created out of the body of a conquered divine being called Tiamat, and human beings are made in order to act as slaves of the gods—a realistic recognition that the life of the human race involves hard work and is often unrewarding. There were indigenous Canaanite versions of this kind of myth, which we are familiar with from the tablets found at Ugarit (Ras Shamra) in Syria, already mentioned above. Israel itself knew and could refer to its own version of the myth, in which the conquered goddess was known as Rahab ('Was it not thou that didst cut Rahab in pieces, that didst pierce the dragon?', Isaiah 51:9).

However, there is a move away from seeing God and the creation in such crudely human terms in both the stories of creation that we encounter in Genesis 1–2. In chapter 2 the creation of the physical world is not described but passed over in a subordinate clause ('In the day that the LORD God made the earth and the heavens', Genesis 2:4), but the creation of human beings is portrayed as being like the work of a potter forming clay, an image also known from Mesopotamia. In Genesis 1, which by general consent is a later account, from the P source, there is no physical contact between God and the world, but it comes into being when God speaks a series of commands ('Let there be … '). It should be noted that this is not in the strict sense a creation out of nothing (*ex nihilo*), since in the beginning there is a watery chaos (Genesis 1:2) which is not directly said to have been created. But it is equally clear that everything of consequence came into being at the divine command. It is not until as late as the second book of Maccabees (second or first century BC) that literal creation out of nothing is categorically affirmed:

> … look at the heaven and the earth and see everything that is in them, and recognize that God did not make them out of things that existed [or, that God made them out of things that did not exist].
>
> (2 Maccabees 7:28)

The general consensus is that it was soon after the exile, probably in the fifth century, that Genesis 1 was written. If so, a major influence on the priestly writer was probably the prophetic figure

Deutero-Isaiah, who is the first Israelite writer to affirm uncondi-
tionally that the God of Israel is the only God in existence, and
hence that the world owes its being to him. Passages such as the
following show Deutero-Isaiah's conception of God.

> The LORD is the everlasting God,
> the creator of the ends of the earth.
> He does not faint or grow weary,
> his understanding is unsearchable.
>
> (Isaiah 40:28)

> I am the LORD, and there is no other,
> besides me there is no God;
> I gird you, though you do not know me,
> that men may know, from the rising of the sun
> and from the west, that there is none besides me;
> I am the LORD, and there is no other.
> I form light and create darkness,
> I make weal and create woe;
> I am the LORD, who do all these things.
>
> (Isaiah 45:5–7)

> For thus says the LORD,
> who created the heavens
> (he is God!),
> who formed the earth and made it
> (he established it;
> he did not create it a chaos,
> he formed it to be inhabited!)
> 'I am the LORD, and there is no other.'
>
> (Isaiah 45:18)

GOD AND HIS CHOSEN PEOPLE

But an important thing to notice here is that the God who is the
sole creator is unequivocally the God of Israel—'the God of
Abraham, Isaac, and Jacob, rather than the God of the philoso-
phers', in Blaise Pascal's famous saying. He is identified as 'the

LORD', that is, as the god YHWH. Nowhere in the Hebrew Bible is the creator God thought of as other than the God known in Israel. This is equally true in the New Testament. The God who is believed by early Christians to have become known more perfectly through Jesus is still the God who both created the universe and chose Israel as a special people. There is no hint anywhere in the New Testament of what would come to be seen as the heresy known as Marcionism, which regards the creator God and the God revealed in Jesus as two separate and opposing forces. Creation and salvation go hand in hand, and it is the same God who is known in both.

This means that both Judaism and Christianity have a certain tension in their conception of God, which we might call a tension between universalism and particularism. Because God is the creator of everything and hence of every human person, nothing and no one can be outside the divine purposes: God must be concerned for all people and all peoples. Yet because the same God is also the God who chose Israel, and in later times added to Israel the non-Israelites who came to make up the majority of members of the church, the God of all is also the God of particular people. Neither religion has completely resolved this tension, veering from time to time and place to place in a more universalist or a more particularist direction. How far, for example, is the *torah* or the Sermon on the Mount meant as an ethical standard for all and how far as instruction for insiders? Are they a universal moral code, or a set of precepts for Jews/Christians who seek perfection? Or when the first letter of John instructs the readers to 'love one another' (1 John 3:11), does this mean that everyone in the world should love everyone else, or that Christians should love their fellow-Christians?

The particularist aspect of God is at the root of what so many people find offensive in 'the Old Testament God', the divine commands to destroy all the native inhabitants of the Promised Land. The book of Joshua contains a great deal about this, and it causes many people to abandon the God of the Bible altogether. There is militant particularism also in the New Testament, where certain people (often, by a certain role-reversal, the Jews) are said to be the object of God's wrath ('God's wrath has come upon them at last!', 1 Thessalonians 2:16). Even when non-Christians are not condemned, it is clear that it is those who truly believe in God through Christ for whom salvation is reserved—this is plain in most of Paul's teaching, despite some universalistic elements. At the same time Paul clearly believed, like the later strands of the Hebrew Bible and like all Jews of his day, that the one God of Israel was also the creator, who had placed all human beings on the earth and had benign purposes for all.

By contrast with the very sketchy hints about the internal nature of God, both Testaments are quite clear that he has a special people as his own. In the Hebrew Bible this results in the telling of the story of Israel as a story of how God first chose himself a people, bore with their waywardness, sometimes acting in mercy and sometimes in vengeance, and will eventually establish them permanently in the land of Israel and bless them irrevocably. In many books the history of Israel is presented as a 'saving history' (*Heilsgeschichte* is the commonly used German word for this), though as we have seen the Deuteronomistic History, taken as a whole, is more a history of sin and failure. In the New Testament the 'people of God' are the Christians: Paul is clear that in so far as they are Gentiles they are 'grafted on' to Israel, and that in the end Israel will be saved along with them (see Romans 11), while other writers seem to think of Israel as having been rejected in favour of Christians (thus possibly the letter to the Hebrews and the Gospel of John). 'Supersessionism', by which the church is seen as having replaced Judaism in the divine scheme of things, is often objected to by Jews and Christians alike today. It is not true that it is ubiquitous in the New Testament, but it is true that some New Testament books do embrace it. Even Paul, who clearly in Romans believes in the eventual salvation of Israel, can talk of 'the Jews' as having killed Jesus and the prophets (1 Thessalonians 2:15) and being under divine wrath. The saving history, for the New Testament writers, is the story of how God raised up Jesus and brought about the creation of the Christian communities that acknowledge him as Saviour: it is in this that the hand of God is to be seen in the world.

THE FIGURE OF JESUS

In the New Testament there is not only a theology but also a *Christology* (or rather several Christologies), that is, an account of the nature of the Christ or Messiah, identified as Jesus of Nazareth.

Until recently, there was a tendency to assume that the earliest Christology in the church was a 'low' one (Jesus seen as Messiah or as a great prophet, but not as divine), and that the kind of 'high' Christology that led to the eventual definitions of Jesus as God in the church's official creeds developed only towards the end of the New Testament period. This follows a common-sense scheme of thought in which it was believed that Jesus was gradually accorded greater and greater honour as Christians moved further and further away from having actually known him in the flesh. We all tend to expect that this is how the veneration of saints and heroes works: it is later generations who see them as more than human, not their contemporaries.

AN EARLY HIGH CHRISTOLOGY?

However, there are reasons to think that this is not how the process worked in the case of Jesus. Some of the highest Christological claims occur in the letters of Paul, written twenty or so years after the crucifixion, and it is the considerably later Gospel of Luke and Acts that on the whole have the lowest Christology in the New Testament. The late first-century John, on the other hand, does certainly have a very high Christology, identifying Jesus with the 'Word' of God, a personified divine attribute akin to Wisdom (see above). The New Testament thus has a wide variety of responses to Jesus, and there is no simple linear development from low to high.

For Paul, the identity and status of Jesus are central, because it is people's reaction to Jesus that determines their own salvation. From a modern perspective one might ask whether people have to put their faith in God or in Jesus. But for Paul this is never an issue: belief in Jesus *is* belief in God, for (as Jesus says in John's Gospel) 'anyone who has seen me has seen the Father' (John 14:9). Paul never says, in so many words, that 'Jesus is God'. What he does say is that 'Jesus is Lord', and he comments that though there may be many lords and many gods for the heathen, for us there is one God and one Lord (see 1 Corinthians 8:5–6). There is no opposition between Jesus and God; they are not alternative objects of devotion. Rather, those who worship the God known in Jesus also worship Jesus. The centrality of Jesus in early Christian worship has been argued as the reason why a Jew such as Paul, who was a strict monotheist, could nevertheless talk of Jesus in divine language: early Christians simply found themselves worshipping Jesus and had to produce a theology (a Christology) that would justify and explain this.

Possibly the highest Christology in Paul is to be found in the so-called 'Christ hymn' in Philippians 2:5–11. There we read:

> Have this mind among yourselves, which you have in Christ Jesus, who, though he was in the form of God, did not count equality with God a thing to be grasped, but emptied himself, taking the form of a servant, being born in the likeness of men. And being found in human form he humbled himself and became obedient unto death, even death on a cross. Therefore God has highly exalted him and bestowed on him the name that is above every name, that at the name of Jesus every knee should bow, in heaven and on earth and under the earth, and every tongue confess that Jesus Christ is Lord, to the glory of God the Father.
> (Philippians 2:5–11)

This is remarkable when we remember that it was composed so soon after the crucifixion of Jesus, and even more remarkable if, as some think, it is actually pre-Pauline, a hymn which Paul is quoting from the early church's worship. It describes Jesus as being 'in the form of God', and seems to see this as part of his status before he was born: thus it may even imply a doctrine of incarnation. It is also possible, however, that it is talking about Jesus as he was in the mind of God, not implying that he actually existed before he was born on earth. Even so, the idea that he was 'in the form of God' makes an enormous claim for his status. At the end of the passage, he is said to have been given the name that is above all names, and there is applied to him a text which in Isaiah is said of God, that every knee shall bend and every tongue confess him (Isaiah 45:23). One could hardly go much further in the direction of seeing Jesus as divine, and certainly not within a monotheistic system, which such language pushes to its limits.

THE GOSPELS

The Synoptic Gospels on the whole claim rather less than this for Jesus, though it is perhaps the earliest, Mark, that claims the most, beginning as it does by describing its contents as the 'gospel of Jesus Christ, the Son of God' (though some manuscripts omit the last phrase). Both Mark and Matthew use a number of important titles for Jesus, including the enigmatic 'Son of man', which may be the title of a heavenly being or angel as it appears to be in the book of Daniel 7, but could also be a less significant idiom meaning simply 'a person'. Both Gospels see Jesus as the promised Messiah. In Luke the Christological titles tend to be 'lower': the centurion at the cross does not say, 'Truly this was the Son of God!' but simply 'Certainly this man was innocent' (Luke 23:47; contrast Matthew 27:54). Much is made of Jesus as a prophet, and the infancy stories play up Jesus' destiny as the Saviour sent to deliver Israel from its woes, but at the expense of seeing him as actually divine, though, as in Matthew, he is miraculously born by a virgin birth through the holy spirit of God. From Luke alone, however, one would probably not conclude that Jesus was divine, and the same is true of Acts, where in Paul's various speeches about him he is portrayed as a man chosen by God to be the Saviour rather than as an incarnation of God himself.

We can see from Hebrews 1, where the author stresses that Jesus is *not* an angel, however an exalted one, that there was an 'angel Christology' in the early church that he felt the need to rebut— possibly one in which Jesus was identified with the archangel Michael or some other powerful angel. Within a Jewish context this was one way of stressing the very high status of Jesus without compromising monotheism, but the author of Hebrews evidently thought it did not go far enough, but that Jesus really bore 'the very stamp of [God's] nature' (Hebrews 1:3), much as in Colossians (possibly not by Paul), where Jesus is 'the image of the invisible God, the first-born of all creation' (Colossians 1:15). The Lukan picture was thus not shared by some of Luke's contemporaries, who wanted a higher Christology.

By general consent the highest New Testament Christology is to be found in John's Gospel, where Jesus discourses at length on his unique relation to his Father, and uses the formula 'I am' which in Deutero-Isaiah characterizes the speech of God himself: most strikingly in the saying, 'Before Abraham was, I am' (John 8:58). The prologue (John 1:1) says that the Word, who was incarnate in Jesus, 'was God'. It avoids using the definite article (*ho theos*) and simply says that the Word was *theos*—we should perhaps translate 'was divine', but just what difference this makes is unclear. It seems to belong to a general wariness in the New Testament to say baldly that 'Jesus is God', while at the same time speaking of him in such a way that he is certainly not *less* than God. In this the later movements of Christological doctrine are anticipated, as Christians tried to remain pure monotheists while at the same time believing that no claim was too high to make about Jesus, whom they worshipped with absolute devotion. The problem has never been fully resolved, and the New Testament writers show us the beginnings of it.

THE TRINITY

Does this mean that the doctrine of the Trinity is already present in the New Testament? Jews and Christians of course differ nowadays on whether there is plurality within God, in particular on whether God is a Trinity as well as a Unity. The Hebrew Bible does not contain any hints in the pluralist direction, despite the occasional passage that the church Fathers took to hint at the Trinity, such as Abraham's three visitors who speak with a single voice (Genesis 18), which is the basis of a well-known icon. It is an important question how far the New Testament is Trinitarian, or whether the development of the doctrine of the Trinity is a wholly post-biblical development. As we have seen, what is said in the New Testament about Jesus often tends in a Trinitarian or at least Binitarian direction. And there are formulas in the New Testament that certainly look Trinitarian. The most obvious is Matthew 28:19, which speaks of the Father, the Son, and the Holy Spirit. But it may be a much later interpolation into manuscripts of the New Testament, deriving from an age when Trinitarian theology was firmly established. More important perhaps is Paul's closing formula in 2 Corinthians 13:14 ('The grace of the Lord Jesus Christ and the love of God and the fellowship of the Holy Spirit be with you all'), and his assertion that in the end all things will be made subject to the Son, and then the Son will be made subject to the Father (1 Corinthians 15:28), which implies at least a Binity, though of what in later ages would have been called a 'subordinationist' kind, in which the Son is not equal to the Father. In general the theology of the New Testament is not overtly Trinitarian though it has suggestions from which Trinitarian theology could be developed.

EVIL IN THE WORLD

In polytheistic religions there is, strictly speaking, no *problem* of evil. Evil things happen because of an imbalance of power among the gods: gods favourable to humans, or to one's own particular people, or to oneself, have been worsted by hostile divine powers, and therefore suffering ensues. Similarly, good things happen when the favourable gods regain the upper hand. For anyone who wishes to look behind the surface of events and see a divine will at work, a polytheistic system is highly satisfactory. There were many peoples in the ancient world, indeed the vast majority, who followed this way of thinking about the events that happened on earth, seeing them as mirroring rivalries and power-struggles among the gods. In classical antiquity Homer's *Iliad* is an eloquent portrayal of this way of thinking, and it lies behind most of the myths produced in Mesopotamia.

THE PROBLEM OF MONOTHEISM

Many people in ancient Israel were also polytheists, and had the same understanding of what happened to them. But there is a thin red line, beginning with the prophets, that chose instead to believe that there was only one divine power, Israel's God Yahweh. For monotheism the problem of evil is far more acute and troubling. If events on earth mirror the divine realm, then that realm, which contains only one God, must somehow include evil within itself. This is the problem discussed with supreme skill in the book of Job. The premiss of the book is that Job is righteous, but his friends try to show that he is really wicked, since only so can God's face be saved when Job falls into horrible suffering. (A less stressed alternative is that God is testing Job to see if he can maintain his innocence in the face of suffering.) In the end their attempts come to nothing and God himself maintains that Job, who has attacked and criticized God, is in the right, whereas his friends, who have tried to 'justify' God, are in the wrong. But in the final speech from the whirlwind God essentially tells both Job and the friends that no attempt to understand his ways can ever succeed: God is inscrutable:

> 'Where were you when I laid the foundations of the earth:
> Tell me, if you have understanding.
> Who determined its measurements—surely you know?
> or who stretched the line upon it?
> On what were its bases sunk,
> or who laid its cornerstone,
> when the morning stars sang together,
> and all the sons of God shouted for joy?'
>
> (Job 38:4–7)

ANGELS AND DEMONS

Later Jewish tradition did not accept the blank sense of incomprehension in the face of life's misfortunes that the book of Job presents. For one thing, in the historical books of the Hebrew Bible it had lengthy expositions of the doctrine that God is *not* inscrutable, but that he can be seen clearly at work in what befalls the nation. For another thing, really strict monotheism, with one power and no more in the heavenly realm, was almost impossible to maintain. We can see from the narrative books that people in early times believed in spirits that might be sent by God to do his dirty work ('the works of his left hand', as Luther was to put it):

> 'I saw the LORD sitting on his throne, and all the host of heaven standing beside him on his right hand and on his left; and the LORD said, "Who will entice Ahab, that he may go up and fall at Ramoth-Gilead?" And one said one thing, and another said another. Then a spirit came forth and stood before the LORD, saying, "I will entice him."
>
> 'And the LORD said to him, "By what means?" And he said, "I will go forth, and will be a lying spirit in the mouth of all his prophets." And he said, "You are to entice him; go forth and do so.'
>
> (1 Kings 22:19–22)

After the Exile there was a whole burgeoning of angels and demons, who acted as God's agents in the world: some think the influence of the Persian religion, Zoroastrianism, is to be seen in this, but it may equally well be an indigenous development, or even a return to a partial polytheism. The figure of Satan, who will make such a vivid appearance in Job, is an example of this development. Where in 1 Samuel 24 David's wicked decision to take a census is attributed to an impulse from God himself, in the later retelling of the story in 1 Chronicles 21 it is Satan who instigates it: implying that by now Satan had a will of his own which was not necessarily an expression of the will of God.

In the New Testament the activity of many angels and evil spirits is taken for granted, and not only bad events but also illness, physical and mental, is attributed to demonic possession. The Sadducees, who 'say that there is no resurrection, nor angels, nor spirit' (Acts 23:8), are regarded as oddities: Paul exploits their disagreement with the Pharisees over this in his speech in Acts 23. Like the many gods of polytheism, angels and demons had enormous explanatory power in accounting for good and bad events. The angels also formed a kind of buffer zone between God and human beings, protecting humankind from being exposed to the sheer raw power of the one and only God and providing means of access, rather like favoured courtiers whom one might cultivate, to the God one would hardly dare to approach without their help. Some of these angels were so mighty that any human being would be in awe of *them* (and might therefore need a more junior go-between!), and among them were certainly the three archangels named in Scripture, Michael, Gabriel, and Raphael. As we have seen, angels provided one model for thinking about the status of Jesus: perhaps he was the incarnation of an archangel?

PUNISHMENT AND TESTING

Alongside explanations of bad events in terms of the work of angels or demons, there lived on the traditions that Job's friends represent: bad things happen to you because you are bad, or perhaps because God wants to test you. The first of these appears in a remarkable passage in John 9:1–3, the beginning of the story of how Jesus healed a man blind from birth, which seems even to toy with the idea of reincarnation. Jesus rejects the explanation of the man's suffering in terms of sin. The second is the usual way of dealing with adversity in all the letters of the New Testament in which suffering is referred to: a trial from God is coming upon his faithful servants, and they must endure, and bear witness to Jesus by the way they endure. Early Christianity took over from the Judaism of its time a strong tradition of martyrdom for the sake of the faith, and many passages in the Epistles and also in the book of Revelation show how pervasive it was:

> Beloved, do not be surprised at the fiery ordeal which come upon you to prove you, as though something strange were happening to you. But rejoice in so far as you share Christ's sufferings, that you may also rejoice and be glad when his glory is revealed. If you are reproached for the name of Christ, you are blessed, because the spirit of glory and of God rests upon you.
>
> (1 Peter 4:12–14)

ESCHATOLOGY

In traditional Christian discourse 'eschatology' refers to the Four Last Things that each person will have to encounter: death, judgement, heaven, and hell (from Greek *eschatos*, meaning 'last'). This scheme does not derive directly from the Bible, and that could mean that we should not use the term eschatology at all in describing biblical themes. But scholars of both Old and New Testaments have found it useful as a way of referring to the hopes and fears for a *decisive future intervention in the world's affairs by God* to which both the Hebrew Bible and the New Testament refer.

PROPHETIC ESCHATOLOGY

In the Hebrew Bible eschatology is at home in the books of the prophets. Prophets in the ancient world were expected to foretell events of concern to the king and the rulers, and the Hebrew prophets, as we saw, were no exception to this. But very often they went beyond their official remit, and declared a degree of disaster for the nation that in its scale went beyond ordinary military success or failure. Amos, classically, foretells the complete downfall of the whole nation, never to recover: 'Fallen, no more to rise, is the virgin Israel' (Amos 5:2). This may well be called an *eschatological* prophecy, since it talks in terms of the end of Israel, not of a setback that might then be followed by a victory. How far the prophets' message in general was eschatological in this sense is a good question: in Hosea and Isaiah, for example, there is (at least as the books now stand) salvation beyond judgement, and so no 'end' of the history of the nation.

Eschatology can however also be positive: God may be bringing national, or world, history to a good climax, after which everyone will be happy and at peace. Deutero-Isaiah's message can be called eschatological in this sense, in that he foretells a restoration of Judah so complete that no trouble will ever assail the nation again. Even the natural order will share in God's blessings, with miraculous fruitfulness making trees flourish and the desert blossom. On the whole, prophecy after the exile continued Deutero-Isaiah's hopeful eschatology: Zechariah for example prophesies that 'Old men and old women shall again sit in the streets of Jerusalem, each with staff in hand for very age' (Zechariah 8:4). But the eschatology of the later parts of the Hebrew Bible never breaks the bounds of earthly reality: in Isaiah 65:20, for example, people still die, even though they live to a very great age ('No more shall there be in [Jerusalem] an infant that lives but a few days, or an old man who does not fill out his days, for the child shall die a hundred years old'). There is little idea of 'heaven', in the sense of somewhere or some state in which people exist after death. Rather inconsistently, the Hebrew Bible tends to say that the fate of the wicked is to go down to Sheol, the Hades-like place of shadows where the dead belong, but not to note that in fact this is the fate of the good, too—a point that Ecclesiastes painfully insists on ('one fate comes to all, to the righteous and the wicked, to the good and the evil, to the clean and the unclean, to him who sacrifices and him who does not sacrifice', Ecclesiastes 9:2). Only in post-biblical Judaism do we find the idea of the resurrection of the righteous to eternal life, though there is a first hint of it in Daniel 12, and some think it may be suggested in Psalms 16:9–11, 17:15, and 49:14–15, as well as in Job 19:26, though all these are uncertain. In the deuterocanonical books of Maccabees, written not long before the New Testament, such a belief is present, however; and the New Testament shows that by the first century AD it was nearly universal among Jews, with the Sadducees notable because they were the exception.

ESCHATOLOGY IN THE NEW TESTAMENT

So by the time of the New Testament, eschatology has this new feature of a concern for the fate of individuals after death. We find it, for example, in Revelation, where the souls of those killed for the sake of Jesus await their vindication (Revelation 6:9–11). We find it in Paul, especially in 1 Corinthians 15, with a long discourse on how the dead are to be raised. Paul as a Pharisee had presumably believed in resurrection before he was converted to Christianity, but the new thing that Christian faith contributed, from his point of view, was that resurrection no longer lay in the distant future. Jesus had *already* been raised, and this was a sign that the last days had begun: believers in Jesus could therefore expect to be raised themselves if they died, and would join those who were still alive at his second coming (see 1 Thessalonians 4:13–18), which was to happen very soon.

But there is also a heavily corporate aspect to New Testament eschatology, just as to that of the Hebrew Bible. Though individual believers would be raised to new life, there was no sense that they were isolated individuals: they were part of the great community of Christians, regarded as a new Israel. The hope for the future in Paul, and among early Christians in general, was thus closer to that of the Old Testament prophets than Christians often think: it continued to have a certain earthy this-worldliness, to be concerned with a world transformed rather than with what Revelation alone in the New Testament describes as a 'new heaven and new earth' (Revelation 21:1; and even there, there is a new *earth*, not simply a new heaven).

One major metaphor the New Testament uses to convey the coming state of affairs in which God will rule over a transformed heaven and earth is the 'kingdom' of God, meaning God's rule as king rather than a place ('heaven'). According to Mark's Gospel, Jesus' own message was that the kingdom of God was about to arrive (this is sometimes called 'imminent eschatology') or even had already begun to dawn ('inaugurated eschatology'). The disciples, similarly, were sent out to proclaim the coming of God's kingdom; and Paul uses 'kingdom' language when he foretells, in 1 Corinthians 15:25, that Christ must 'reign until he has put all his enemies under his feet'.

Complicating the matter further is the existence in the New Testament of what is usually called 'realized eschatology'—the belief that the 'last things' have already arrived and can be seen in the transformed lives of believers. There is probably no New Testament book that wholly ignores the future; but in some, notably the Gospels of Luke and John, there is an emphasis on the fact that (as Jesus puts it in Luke 17:21) 'the kingdom of God is within you/among you', in other words the eagerly expected rule of God can already be seen at work in the way Christians live their lives. It is possible to hold a completely realized eschatology, in which one has no expectation of future divine intervention at all, but sees the present life as the arena where God is to be encountered, and there are probably many Christians today who embrace such a belief. But the New Testament as a whole does not support such an idea, and indeed it may be that it was this idea that Paul had in mind when he condemned those who thought the kingdom had already arrived (2 Thessalonians 2:2, if this is by Paul). Nevertheless there are traces of it in the New Testament, and John's Gospel, for example, makes so much of the idea that the glory of God is finally revealed in the cross that it seems to leave little logical room for either the resurrection or the future coming of God in glory. Yet even here there are in fact predictions of the coming kingdom; and John has some of the most vivid resurrection narratives. There is probably no total consistency about questions of eschatology in the New Testament, just as nowadays Jews and Christians have very varied expectations of what follows death, often combining a belief in the immortality of the soul with hope for the resurrection of the body, and a concern for what happens to each individual after they die with hope for a renewal of the whole world. These are speculative questions to which believers do not have a single unified solution, and nor did they in the first century.

ETHICS

The Bible has a great deal to say about how human beings ought to live. The Jewish designation of the Pentateuch, and sometimes by extension of the whole Hebrew Bible, as *torah* (teaching) shows that in the Jewish community the ethical side of the Bible is very much to the fore. Christians have tended to concentrate on other aspects, but for them too the Bible is a major source of moral teaching.

ETHICS IN THE HEBREW BIBLE

In the Hebrew Bible there are many prescriptive texts, mainly in the legal material already surveyed. Perhaps the typical legal material is to be found in the Ten Commandments, which lay down a list of (mainly) prohibitions dealing with basic human conduct, such as can be found in the religious teaching of other nations and other religions: rules forbidding murder, theft, and adultery, for example, can be found all over the world. At the same time even the Ten Commandments contain one specifically Jewish command, to keep the Sabbath—this is one of two positive Commandments, the other being to honour one's parents. And the opening injunction to have no other gods than Yahweh is also peculiar to Israelite culture: most nations in the ancient Near East lacked any sense that there were gods who should be worshipped uniquely. Nevertheless the Ten Commandments do encapsulate a moral vision that draws on some universal human insights into ethics. This is not the case with the detailed ritual legislation that takes up most of Leviticus, which is uniquely Israelite.

It is natural to look at the 'law' first when studying the ethical insights of the Hebrew Bible, but there are three other sources that should not be overlooked: wisdom, prophecy, and narrative. The wisdom literature contains a lot of ethical teaching, though it is presented as the advice of a teacher rather than as the direct command of God. The prophets talk about morality in terms of what the people should have done but have failed to do, or have done when they ought not to have done it, rather than giving positive advice or orders, but from this we can of course easily see how they thought the people they address ought to be living. Narrative texts are trickier, because it is often not easy to discern which courses of action the narrator is describing with approval and which with disapproval. But sometimes we get value-judgements on particular characters in the story ('King X did what was evil in the sight of the LORD'), or it is clear from the way the story is told that we are meant to approve or disapprove of the actions described.

ETHICS IN THE NEW TESTAMENT

In the New Testament there are two main sources for ethics: the recorded teaching of Jesus, particularly in continuous texts such as the Sermon on the Mount in Matthew 5–7, and the ethical instruction in the Letters, especially those of Paul. Here the term 'moral vision' has been used helpfully to point out that we seldom have law-like moral teaching, but more often a sketch of the ideal Christian life. In the case of the Sermon on the Mount there has been a debate over how literally the extremely demanding moral precepts are intended to be followed. To take an example, it is easy to see what is meant by a command not to commit adultery, which is found in the Ten Commandments and endorsed in Jesus' own teaching. But when Jesus condemns even lustful looks, is that meant to imply that anyone who looks with desire at a person to whom they are not married is equally guilty; and what consequences would be expected to follow?

For many Christians this teaching has been taken with absolute literalness, resulting (if one applies the same principle to other sins) in a very demanding moral code. For others, Jesus is here setting out an ideal, which he does not expect most people to attain. The more rigorist reading, indeed, can itself be taken in one of two ways: as meaning that the Christian life requires enormous self-control and the highest possible moral standards, or (and this has been common in Lutheran interpretation) as intended to make us realize that God's standards of morality are ultimately unfulfillable, and hence throw us back on divine mercy and grace. If you were to be perfect, this is what you would have to do, but that only shows how impossible it is for you ever to be perfect, and consequently how much in need you are of a salvation that can come about only through God's free gift. Another variant is the theory that the Sermon on the Mount represents an 'interim ethic'—incredibly high standards, but standards that Christians were only expected to keep between now and the imminent end.

Paul's moral teaching undoubtedly does contain some interim ethics, as he himself spells out. His advice (overtly presented as advice rather than divine command) that it is better to remain celibate is 'in view of the impending distress' (1 Corinthians 7:26).

With the end about to come, it is not the time to be contracting a marriage and having to spend time on domestic concerns when one should be concentrating on the things of God. One of the changes one notices in the deutero-Pauline Pastoral Letters is that Christians are now living without this imminent expectation, and are settling into normal married life and setting up systems for caring for the needy, widows, and so on. The loss of the sense of an imminent end is one of the things that mark these letters off from the genuine Pauline ones. But Paul himself does issue some short digests of how Christians ought to behave, generally towards the ends of his letters, and these have a striking 'moral vision', concentrating on joy, harmony among believers, peaceableness towards outsiders, and sympathy for everyone:

> The fruit of the Spirit is love, joy, peace, patience, kindness, goodness, faithfulness, gentleness, self-control.
>
> (Galatians 5:22)

SECT OR NATION?

The New Testament was written for 'insiders' in a new movement, only just beginning to separate from Judaism and to become a separate religion, and its ethical teaching, accordingly, says nothing about how human beings in general should live. Non-Christians are not reading this literature, and would not take any notice of it if they did. Things are rather different with the Hebrew Bible. True, it is written for those who belong to 'Israel'—inhabitants of the land of Israel in early times, and Jews both in Israel and in the wider Dispersion in later time. But it is the literature of a whole nation, not of a small sect, and therefore naturally covers more areas of ethical concern, whereas the New Testament tends to concentrate on matters of personal morality and of relationships within the Christian community.

One obvious difference is that the Hebrew Bible has a lot of material on the taking of human life, since it has to legislate for a nation that had some kind of judicial system. There is nothing like this in the New Testament: early Christians did not have the power to try legal cases or to inflict penalties on offenders. The Hebrew Bible has an attitude to the taking of human life that is unusual in the ancient world. All murder (i.e. deliberate homicide) is a capital offence. This differs from the norms in some of the surrounding cultures, as can be seen from the *Code of Hammurabi*. Here the penalty for murder depends on the relative social status of the victim and the murderer: killing a slave is not treated as seriously as killing a nobleman. It follows that not all murderers are executed. But one could argue that the Hebrew Bible's requirement that execution, not a fine, is the only acceptable penalty for murder, regardless of the status of the people involved, represents a higher valuation of human life. This may be connected with the idea that humans are made 'in the image and likeness of God' (Genesis 1:26–27), and this principle is explicitly stated in the clearest reference to the death penalty for murder, Genesis 9:6.

Similarly, the Hebrew Bible contains complex and detailed property laws, which the writers of the New Testament were in no position to do anything about, though Paul seems to wish they were, exhorting his readers to settle disputes among themselves rather than going to the secular law courts (1 Corinthians 6:1–8). In the Hebrew Bible there is a close link between respect for people's life and respect for their property. Theft of course is forbidden in the Ten Commandments, but the laws cover also more subtle forms of taking other people's property. Property given into someone else's safekeeping may not be embezzled:

> If a man delivers to his neighbour an ass or an ox or a sheep or any beast to keep, and it dies or is hurt or is driven away, without anyone seeing, an oath by the LORD shall be between them to see whether he has not put his hand to his neighbour's property.
>
> (Exodus 22:10–11)

In effect this probably refers to a form of banking. If a banker says that your money or goods have gone missing, he will need to prove he hasn't taken them himself. The prophets also condemn theft, especially theft of land. There seems to have been a principle in Israel that ancestral land could not be alienated: the owner could not sell it, much less anyone else seize it by force (Micah 2:2). This can also be illustrated from one of the narratives in Kings, the story of Naboth's vineyard (1 Kings 21), where King Ahab wants a patch of Naboth's land and, when he refuses, citing this principle, Ahab's wife Jezebel contrives to get Naboth executed on a trumped-up charge so that his property will revert to the crown.

Fair practice in commercial dealings is another concern in the Hebrew Bible, hardly mirrored in the New Testament. The prophets particularly condemn corrupt commercial practice:

> Hear this, you who trample upon the needy,
> and bring the poor of the land to an end,
> saying, 'When will the new moon be over,
> that we may sell grain?
> and the sabbath,
> that we may offer wheat for sale?
> that we may make the ephah small and the shekel great,
> and deal deceitfully with false balances?'

> (Amos 8:4–5)

The ephah is a measure of volume, so using a small ephah means that customers get less than they paid for, while the shekel is a measure of weight, used to weigh the customer's silver—a larger one means that more money is being exacted from the customer than the agreed price. Fair weights and measures are a frequent concern in the Hebrew Bible—cf. Deuteronomy 25:13–16 and Proverbs 11:1, 16:11, and 20:10. The Hebrew Bible also has a great concern for fairness and equity in legal practice. Even under foreign powers, Israel probably retained its own legal system, and was concerned that it should be administered fairly. The Hebrew Bible's constant rebuke of bribery no doubt means that this was fairly common, as it is in most societies. The New Testament church of course was not competent to try cases in court, and depended on Roman justice in major matters and on Jewish justice for more narrowly religious cases. Not until the church began to be dominant in Mediterranean society did it start to be involved in public justice.

RELIGION AND SEX

There are two ethical areas in which both the Hebrew Bible and the New Testament have plentiful material: religious practice and sexual morality. As we have seen, the Hebrew Bible has page after page of legislation about how worship is to be conducted, with detailed definitions of types of sacrifice and religious festivals. A modern Christian perspective tends to think that these are not matters of 'ethics' but of ritual. The distinction however is foreign to Judaism, and was certainly not made by most of the authors of the Hebrew Bible, for whom the obligation to offer sacrifices at festivals is on all fours with the obligation to honour one's parents or to avoid the worship of other gods. Even wisdom writers, who do sometimes suggest that 'ethics' is more important than 'cult', nevertheless stress that sacrifices should still be offered. Thus Proverbs 21:3 says that 'to do righteousness and justice is more acceptable to the LORD than sacrifice', but this is balanced by 3:9–10, which exhorts the reader to 'honour the LORD with your substance and with the first fruits of all your produce'. Only in the pre-exilic prophets do we find condemnation of religious ritual, which they think people are using as a substitute for the more demanding task of living rightly in society (see Amos 5:21–24 and Isaiah 1:10–20).

The New Testament provides only very sketchy evidence about early Christian worship, but Paul recalls the institution of the Eucharist in words that show it was already what a modern Christian would recognize as such (1 Corinthians 11:23–26), and he discusses baptism, though in a rather ambivalent way. On the one hand it is crucial that Christians are baptized, since baptism (like circumcision for Jews) indicates membership of the community and can even be seen as symbolizing dying and rising with Christ. On the other hand, he seems rather uninterested in whether he baptized this or that person in Corinth, saying that God did not send him to baptize but to preach the gospel (see 1 Corinthians 1:14–17). Of other types of worship we learn little. Paul himself, in 1 Corinthians 14, gives a sketchy account of what happened in worship at Corinth: hymns, prayers, prophecies, speaking in tongues, and interpretation of what is said, but perhaps no reading of Scripture (at least, this is not mentioned). There is nothing corresponding to the profusion of detail about worship we find in the Hebrew Bible.

On sexual morality both Testaments have a good deal to say. We have already discussed Jesus' condemnation of 'adultery in the heart'. He also pronounced on the question of divorce, apparently giving a stricter ruling than most Jewish teachers of his day—that is, one that in context safeguarded the wife more against summary divorce by her husband, though the details of his teaching are obscured by textual difficulties in the relevant verses (Matthew 19:3–12, Mark 10:2–12). The Hebrew Bible is notably more lenient towards husbands who wish to divorce their wives (Deuteronomy 24:1–4), but makes no provision for a wife to divorce her husband, as Roman law did in the time of Jesus. Paul seems to assume that divorce is possible, since he discusses whether believers ought to seek divorce from unbelieving partners—his judgement is that it is better that they should not, but not that it is forbidden (1 Corinthians 7). Remarriage after divorce is discussed by Jesus and apparently forbidden; Paul says nothing about it.

Homosexual relations between men are forbidden in Leviticus (20:13) and deplored by Paul (Romans 1:27), as they are in some other ancient Near Eastern codes but, as is well known, not in ancient Greece or Rome. Homosexual relations between women are nowhere mentioned in the Hebrew Bible, but are condemned in just one verse in Romans (1:26). The Hebrew Bible's language of 'abomination' used for male-on-male anal intercourse ('lying with a man as with a woman') is a strong condemnation, though there are no cases in narrative books where the issue occurs: the crime of Sodom is clearly, in context, the threat of homosexual *rape* (Genesis 19), not consensual sex between men (see also Judges 19 for a terrible example of the gang-rape of a man's concubine, substituted for a male visitor whom the local inhabitants wish to rape). Paul hints at various shameful deeds not fit to be mentioned (Ephesians 5:12, though this may not be Pauline) but (consistently) does not tell us what they were. It seems that he found the culture of many Greek cities, and perhaps especially Corinth, full of immorality from his Jewish perspective, just as did the writer of 1 John ('all that is in the world, the lust of the flesh and the lust of the eyes and the pride of life, is not of the Father', 1 John 2:16).

SOCIAL ORDER IN PAUL

Despite Paul's sense that the time was short, he did issue instructions as to how members of Christian households should conduct themselves, and these are to be found in the so-called *Haustafeln* (household tables) that end several of the letters. In them Paul proves to be socially quite conservative: slaves, for example, are expected to obey their masters despite the fact that in Christ there is 'neither slave nor free' (Galatians 3:28). There is also 'neither male nor female', yet women are expected to keep to a subordinate place, treating their husbands with respect. On the other hand Paul does give instructions as to how they are to behave when they speak in the Christian assembly (1 Corinthians 11:5 and 11:13), which seems to conflict with his advice elsewhere that they should remain silent (1 Corinthians 14:33–34); some scholars suspect that the text has been tampered with to claw back male privilege. On the whole feminist writers have seen in Paul someone who for his time was remarkably affirming of women's role, as there seems little doubt that Jesus himself had been; of course he could not fall entirely out of his cultural matrix, but within it he espoused rather liberal positions.

FAITH AND GRACE

Paul above all other writers has been central to much biblical study, especially among Protestants and above all among Lutherans, for whom the Pauline gospel is *the* gospel. Central to this gospel as presented in Protestant tradition is the doctrine of justification through faith, or better, by grace through faith. The 'good news' that Paul proclaimed was, according to this interpretation, that through Christ God declares the ungodly (which is to say, everyone) acceptable to himself, just as if they had deserved it, when in fact no one can deserve God's grace since 'all have sinned, and fallen short of the glory of God' (Romans 3:23). Ethical systems in Christianity, such as the Sermon on the Mount (see above), have as their purpose not to provoke obedience, but to show us just how impossible obedience is: how far we fall short of what God wants us to be and therefore how much our salvation depends only on his freely given love.

Now Paul develops this idea through a contrast with the Jewish law or *torah*. In Galatians and in more detail in Romans he seeks to show that the law cannot be kept, it is simply too demanding. If the law had been such that one could keep it fully, then righteousness would have been attainable through such a law; but the

Jewish law as it stands is unkeepable. No one is made righteous through the 'deeds of the law', because no one can observe them adequately. That being so, God cannot have issued the law as the precondition of salvation, since he must have known no-one would ever be able to qualify. The law was given to show us just how far human beings fall short of God's demands, and so to throw them back on God's grace and mercy. All who accept that mercy through faith in Jesus Christ are immediately acquitted of their sins and promised eternal life.

THE LUTHERAN INTERPRETATION OF PAUL

In traditional Lutheran interpretation Paul is seen as an adversary of Judaism, which stands for the whole system that God has over-thrown in Christ, the religion of demand and of merit. Judaism (like Catholicism, to which in many ways this interpretation assimilates it) is seen as a religion in which people *earn* their salva-tion through strenuous moral activity, and in which God is con-strained to bless them because they deserve it. Against that, it is said, Paul puts forward a religion based on pure grace, in which God is infinitely generous to the undeserving, and any attempt to please him by 'good works' shows that one is not relying on faith alone and so is not a true believer. This produces the paradoxical idea that those who strive hardest to please God may actually be the worst Christians; and it raises awkward questions about whether in that case Christianity makes any moral demands at all, or if so whether it matters whether one keeps them. It can easily lead to *antinomianism*, the belief that Christians are entirely free from behaving morally. Paul himself faces this possible implication of his teaching, asking 'Are we to continue in sin that grace may abound?' (Romans 6:1). He replies in the negative, as also do all good Lutherans. But the fact that the question arises shows, it is suggested, that he really does place a very heavy emphasis on the free grace of God, and really does downplay the importance of moral obedience.

THE 'NEW PERSPECTIVE ON PAUL'

In recent times there has developed a different way of interpreting all this, usually known as the New Perspective on Paul (NPP). This has two central elements. One is the belief that Judaism has been misinterpreted, whether by Paul or by Lutheran theologians. The idea of Judaism as a religion of merit, it is now said, is a caricature. Of course Judaism is not antinomian—but nor is any brand of Christianity, in practice. Everyone agrees that God lays on human beings commandments that they are under an obligation to abide by. But Judaism does not (and did not in the first century) suppose that human obedience binds God's hands, as though one could force him to bless or that he is kind only to the deserving. The Hebrew Bible often spells out that salvation comes through God's free grace ('Know therefore that the LORD your God is not giving you this good land to possess because of your righteousness', Deuteronomy 9:6). But in granting this grace he also graciously grants a covenant, a binding agreement between himself and Israel, and Jews have the duty (which is also a privilege) of remaining within the covenant by obeying the commandments of the *torah*:

> And now, Israel, what does the LORD your God require of you, but to fear the LORD your God, to walk in all his ways, to love him, to serve the LORD your God with all your heart and with all your soul?
>
> (Deuteronomy 10:12)

God's faithfulness to Israel, which is undeserved, is guaranteed, but each individual must remain true to the covenant by observing the 613 precepts of the *torah*, as they are counted in modern Orthodox Judaism. And they are all keepable: the idea that the law cannot be kept is a fair comment on such exaggerated demands as those in the Sermon on the Mount, but quite unfair when applied to the Jewish *torah*, which is 'in your mouth and in your heart, so that you can do it' (Deuteronomy 30:14). It is a travesty of the *torah* to speak as if it was a means for earning salvation: it is, rather, the grateful and delighted response of someone who recognizes God's free salvation.

This interpretation knocks away one of the mainstays of the account of Paul's thought given above. If Paul taught that, then he misunderstood the very Judaism in which he had been brought up and educated. But the second element in the NPP is to question whether it is conceivable that Paul, the Orthodox Jew, could possibly have so misunderstood his own ancestral religion. After all, at the same time as Paul questioned the importance of 'works of the law', he also issued his converts and disciples in the churches with detailed moral instructions, and warned them that certain activities would put them outside the kingdom of God: 'those who do such things cannot inherit the kingdom of God' (Galatians 5:21). This strongly suggests that his system was more a Christian version of Judaism than Judaism's polar opposite. Salvation comes by grace, but the response to grace lies in moral obedience, and salvation can be forfeited even though it cannot be earned in the first place. The key to being able to read Paul along these lines lies in analysing more closely his phrase 'the works of the law', which has wrongly been taken to mean moral obedience to God's requirements. In fact the 'works of the law' are those specifically Jewish rules that mark the Jew off from the Gentile: not right social and sexual conduct, which of course God requires, but circumcision, sabbath-keeping, the whole sacrificial cultus, the food laws, and so on. It is *these* things that are not required of Gentile Christians. (Jews today equally believe that they are not binding on anyone but Jews.) Seen in this way, Paul's argument makes sense in a very specific context, the raging debate in the early church over whether Gentiles needed to become Jews before they could become Christians. Paul, against various other Christian teachers, believed fervently that salvation was offered to Gentiles 'without the works of the law', that is, without their having to take on the burden of obeying all the precepts of the *torah*. They need not be circumcised, for example, or keep the food laws. Acts 15 records a debate about this issue in the early church, at which Paul's party won the day; Acts 10 tells us that Peter himself had become convinced of the same thing through a vision, though Galatians 1:11–21 suggests he may have backslidden.

The NPP has the potential to reduce tension between Judaism and Christianity over the doctrine of 'justification by faith alone', just as it might also help to lead to some reconciliation between Protestants and Catholics. If Paul was radical, it was in declaring that the covenant between God and Israel was henceforth open to Gentiles without their having to live as Jews. But he did not mean to suggest that it did not matter how they lived at all: *of course* they must continue to keep the basic moral law, what rabbinic Judaism would come to call the 'Noachite law', a summary of basic morality supposed to have been revealed to all humankind after the Flood.

Another factor in the NPP is that it also reduces the contrast between Paul and James, which we alluded to in chapter 1. James's idea that faith without works is dead is true, if by 'works' we mean 'living well'; and Paul's idea that works are not necessary where there is faith is also true, if by 'works' we mean specifically Jewish religious rules. The contradiction arises from taking the phrase in the same way in the two letters. James is evidence, however, as also is 2 Peter 3:15–16, that Paul was widely misunderstood and found difficult in the next generation; so modern commentators are not wholly to blame if they too have found it hard to understand him.

All that being said, Paul's doctrine of salvation by grace alone remains central to the Christian message, even if it is not as original as Christians sometimes think, being anticipated in Judaism and in the religious thought of ancient Israel, as the references above to Deuteronomy show. One of the religious insights of the Bible, in both Testaments, is that the relation between God and humankind is not symmetrical. 'God will love you if you love God' is not simply an oversimplification, it is a misunderstanding of the difference between God and human beings. God's demands always follow from his love. This is an idea which unites, rather than divides, Judaism and Christianity.

FURTHER READING

There are surprisingly few good books on the nature of God in the Bible. Most relevant material can be found in Theologies of the Old or New Testament, such as Walter Brueggemann, *Theology of the Old Testament: Testimony, Dispute, Advocacy*, Minneapolis: Fortress, 1997.

Christology in the New Testament is surveyed in Catrin H. Williams, 'Interpretation of the Identity and Role of Jesus', in John Barton (ed.), *The Biblical World*, vol. 2, London: Routledge, 2002. For longer treatments see J. D. G. Dunn, *Christology in the Making: A New Testament Inquiry into the Origins of the Doctrine of the Incarnation*, London: SCM, 1989 (second edition). For the theory of an early high Christology see especially Larry Hurtado, *One God, One Lord: Early Christian Devotion and Ancient Jewish Monotheism*, Edinburgh: T & T Clark, 1998 (second edition).

There is a useful collection of articles on the 'problem of evil' in the Old Testament: James L. Crenshaw, *Theodicy in the Old Testament*, London: SPCK, 1983.

For biblical eschatology books on prophecy, apocalyptic, and Paul all offer insights. John J. Collins, *The Apocalyptic Imagination: An Introduction to Jewish Apocaliptic Literature*, Grand Rapids, Mich.: Eerdmans, 1998 (second edition), is particularly useful. On New Testament eschatology in particular see N. T. Wright, *The Climax of the Covenant: Christ and the Law in Pauline Theology*, Edinburgh: T & T Clark, 1991, and *Jesus and the Victory of God*, London: SPCK, 1996, both of which have extensive bibliographies.

There is not much good and accessible material on ethics in the Old Testament, but an accessible approach on the basis of a Christian commitment is provided in C. J. H. Wright, *Old Testament Ethics for the People of God*, Leicester: Inter-varsity Press, 2004. See also John Barton, *Ethics and the Old Testament*, London: SCM Press, second edition 2002. For the New Testament the outstanding work is Richard B. Hays, *The Moral Vision of the New Testament*, Edinburgh: T & T Clark, 1997.

For the 'new perspective on Paul' there is a collection of essays by J. D. G. Dunn, *The New Perspective on Paul: Collected Essays*, Tübingen: Mohr Siebeck, 2005, in which the progress of the debate can be followed. See also Heikki Räisänen, *Paul and the Law*, Tübingen: Mohr, 1983.

THE BIBLE AND HISTORY

5

The popular attitude to the Bible is that it is largely a book of historical records, but that these records are almost entirely fictitious. Neither of these assumptions is justified. As we have already seen, a great deal of the Bible is not historiographical in character at all: alongside the great narrative works such as Samuel, Kings, or the Gospels, it also contains aphoristic wisdom, poetry, prophecy, letters, and apocalypses. But it is also not the case that the Bible is substantially a work of fiction, and that only 'believers' are likely to find in it material worthy of acceptance as historically important.

The Bible contains many references to people and events that are attested in other sources. In the New Testament it speaks of Pontius Pilate, the emperor Tiberius, various Jewish figures such as Gamaliel, and Jesus and Paul themselves, who may be the subject of later embroidery but are certainly historical figures. In the Old Testament some of the kings of Israel are attested in contemporary documents: King Jehu, for example, appears on an Assyrian monument known as the Black Obelisk, and Sennacherib and Nebuchadnezzar are known from innumerable Assyrian and Babylonian sources, while Antiochus Epiphanes and his opponents, the Maccabees, are certainly not fictitious. Whether what is said about these figures and others like them is in fact historically accurate is an important question, which we shall examine in this chapter; but to regard the biblical account as pure folklore or fairy-tale is a genre-mistake.

HISTORY AND THE HEBREW BIBLE

The narrative books in the Old Testament form a complete whole, covering history from creation (Genesis) until the reign of a Persian king called Artaxerxes (Esther). But where the books of Maccabees are included in the canon, there is scriptural information also about the Hellenistic age of the last two centuries BC.

THE HISTORY OF ISRAEL: TRADITIONAL ACCOUNT

Genesis 1–11 is about the early history of the whole world, but thereafter the narrative narrows down to Abraham, presented as living in the second millennium BC, and his descendants. Abraham, it tells us, came from Mesopotamia, ultimately from Ur, which lies in the area that was once the land of Sumer, near to the Persian Gulf. He settled in the land of Canaan, and his son Isaac and grandson Jacob lived there and obtained wives from their kinsfolk, who by now were living in Syria. In the next generation Joseph was sold as a slave into Egypt through the malice of his brothers, who bear the names of the later tribes of Israel; but he prospered in Egypt and was able to settle his brothers and their families there, so that for some generations the descendants of Abraham lived comfortably in Egypt.

When a later Egyptian ruler oppressed the Hebrews, they were rescued from Egypt through the actions of Moses, who had grown up at the Egyptian court. They fled from Egypt, crossed the Red Sea, where the pursuing Egyptians were drowned, wandered in the desert south of Canaan for forty years, and then entered it across the Jordan from the east, destroying many cities as they took possession of the land. After the death of Moses' successor Joshua they were ruled for some time by 'judges', but eventually under the leadership of Samuel they opted to have a king like other nations of the time. Saul was chosen; when he failed, David came to the throne, and established a dynasty. His son Solomon created a wealthy empire stretching well beyond the borders of Palestine: this according to the biblical dating must have been somewhere in the tenth century BC.

On Solomon's death the kingdom divided into the two states of Israel in the north and Judah in the south. The north, larger and more prosperous, was also politically less stable, and there were frequent *coups d'état* there. In the eighth century it was swept away by the Assyrians, who turned it into an Assyrian province. Judah continued in being with mixed fortunes until it too was destroyed, this time by the Babylonians, and all the significant leaders—king, priests, and officials—were taken into exile in Babylonia. Some fifty years later the Persian king Cyrus, who had conquered Babylon, allowed some of the exiles to return, and they established a new state and rebuilt the ruined Temple. There were reform movements led by Ezra and Nehemiah, Jewish officials who were allowed to return to Judah for the purpose. Apart from the story of Esther, who saved the Jews in Persia from persecution, the Hebrew Bible tells us no more about the history of Israel, though the books of the Maccabees pick up the story after a gap of about three centuries and relate the oppression of the Jews in Jerusalem by the Hellenistic king Antiochus Ephiphanes, and the successful campaign waged against him by the freedom-fighters known as the Maccabees.

CRITICAL ASSESSMENT

The Old Testament thus purports to recount human history from the creation, and obviously the earlier stages of its account must be regarded as myth or legend rather than as historiography. The interesting question for the student of the Bible is whether there is a point in the biblical story at which legend gives way to at least source-material for historical reconstruction, even if the texts are not themselves history writing as we understand it. Fashion in biblical studies swings to and fro on this issue. In the late nineteenth century there was considerable scepticism about the historicity of any recorded events earlier than the time of David and Solomon (possibly eleventh or tenth century BC). By the middle years of the twentieth century, on the other hand, it had become normal to regard the 'patriarchal age', the time of Abraham, Isaac, and Jacob and their immediate descendants (perhaps late second millennium), as a real historical period, with Moses and the exodus from Egypt as lying very much in the realm of 'real history'. At the moment, an influential movement generally known as minimalism is sceptical about any time before the Persian period (late sixth century onwards), with the more extreme minimalists thinking that almost all of the Old Testament was composed as late as the Hellenistic Age (late fourth century onwards) and hence does indeed (as in the popular mind) represent largely fiction. There exists a kind of mediating position, for which it is the eighth century that marks the point at which we touch 'real' history, and it is that view on the whole that we shall follow here.

But to the minimalists must be conceded that nineteenth-century study made a major breakthrough in demolishing the assumption that anything recorded in the Bible must have happened more or less as described, and it is vital not to lose sight of this insight. W. M. L. de Wette (1780–1849) was perhaps the first to write a history of ancient Israel that did not simply follow the biblical account, supplementing it from other known records (sparse at that time) and reconciling discrepancies. From his work onwards, biblical scholars have adopted a critical attitude to the biblical sources for the history of Israel, recognizing that much of what the Bible asserts does indeed lie in the realm of legend, especially for earlier periods. As developed by Julius Wellhausen (1844–1918) in the 1870s, this way of looking at the history of Israel is deeply sceptical of anything before the rise of the monarchy. It is conceded that some of Israel's ancestors may have come into the Land from further east, as the stories of Abraham and his family in Genesis imply, and that others may have come from Egypt, as in the stories of Moses and the exodus in the book of Exodus; though it is not clear that one of these groups preceded the other as the Bible implies—the 'patriarchal' migrations from Mesopotamia and/or Syria could be contemporary with the settlement of the land by people from Egypt. But this is a far cry from saying that Abraham or even Moses were real people about whom we can make any historical assertions. Rather, they are folk-heroes about whom later Israelites spun tales, attributing to them ideas and experiences that were really their own.

Nineteenth-century scholars did not exhibit the same scepticism when it came to the stories of the kings and prophets: from David or Solomon onwards, they assumed, the Bible records events in something like the way they actually happened, and for the first

Figure 2 TRADITIONAL DATINGS OF PERSONS AND EVENTS IN THE HEBREW BIBLE

Century BC	
Pre-13th	The patriarchs: Abraham, Isaac, Jacob, Joseph
13th	The Exodus and entry into the Promised Land: Moses and Joshua
12th	The judges
11th	Saul and David
10th	Solomon; division of the nation into Israel and Judah
9th	The dynasty of Omri in the northern kingdom
8th	Jeroboam I in Israel, Uzziah in Judah. Prophets Amos, Hosea, Isaiah, and Micah. Fall of northern kingdom to Assyria
7th	Prophets Jeremiah and Habakkuk. Fall of Assyria to the Babylonians
6th	Babylonian capture of Jerusalem in 597: beginning of the exile. Prophets Ezekiel and Deutero-Isaiah. Fall of Babylonian empire to Cyrus: beginning of Persian empire. Prophets Haggai, Zechariah, Trito-Isaiah
5th	Israel under Persian domination: prophet Malachi. Judah ruled by high priests
4th	Fall of Persian empire to Alexander the Great: beginning of Hellenistic age in Judah
2nd	Maccabean revolt against Antiochus Epiphanes: beginning of Hasmonean dynasty

Most scholars now think that all events noted in the Hebrew Bible before the ninth century are very doubtful.

time real dating is possible. A central point of accurate dating is provided by the biblical account of an invasion by the Egyptian Pharaoh Shishak (Sheshonq) in 1 Kings 14:25–28, where we know from Egyptian records that the date must have been around 918 BC. From then on the books of Kings provide a real chronology for the regnal years of the kings of Judah and Israel—real, not in the sense that it is necessarily infallibly accurate, but in that it is not obviously made up of purely symbolic numbers, and has general plausibility.

The twentieth century saw a slow back-pedalling from this rather sceptical position, largely under the influence of 'biblical archae-ology'. Archaeology was carried out in Palestine from the work of A. H. Layard (1817–94) onwards, but in the mid-twentieth century it boomed. Broadly speaking it was undertaken by German and American archaeologists. The German approach was rather cool in its spirit, open to correlation between archaeological discoveries and the biblical text but not disposed to challenge the historically scep-tical character of German scholarship on biblical history: Martin Noth (1902–68), for example, saw no reason to think that Moses was a real historical figure—or, if he was, he was one about whom virtually nothing could be known. Archaeology did not contribute materially to this kind of question. American scholars, on the other hand, became much more sanguine about the possibility of real historical knowledge, digging with the overt aim of illustrating and if possible confirming the biblical record. Three American archae-ological/biblical scholars to whom what came to be known as 'biblical archaeology' owed most were W. F. Albright (1891–1971), G. E. Wright (1909–74), and John Bright (1909–95). In their hands archaeological work became a major means of revalidating the biblical record, and in their works Abraham, Moses, and Joshua became once more real people about whom something definite could be known.

ANCIENT TEXTS OUTSIDE THE BIBLE

Some of the most important archaeological finds of the twentieth century have been not artefacts but texts, and it was on ancient texts that the biblical archaeologists rested their case for a much greater confidence in the Bible's own account of Israel's history. Second-millennium texts from two sites—ancient Nuzi and ancient

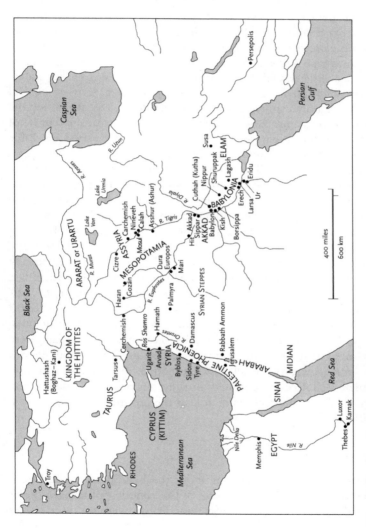

Figure 3 The Near East in ancient times

Mari—both in Mesopotamia, recorded social customs at odds with what was normal in Israel for most of the first millennium, yet strikingly parallel to those in the stories of the patriarchs. Examples are the marriage of siblings (cf. Genesis 20) and the adoption of slaves by childless couples (cf. Genesis 15:2). Perhaps even more striking were the names found in these texts, which were often of the same type as those of the Hebrew patriarchs, and unlike those recorded in later Old Testament books. All this was felt to undermine Wellhausen's image of the patriarchal age as what he had called a 'glorified mirage' projected back from later times, for the practices and names now brought to light were clearly *not* those of later Israel, but might genuinely go back into the period the Bible implies, the mid-second millennium BC.

Suddenly the Old Testament record began to look much more plausible, and nineteenth-century German scepticism about the biblical account started to seem thinly rationalistic. Among the tribes now known to have migrated across the Middle East perhaps there really were people called Abraham, Isaac, and Jacob, doing much what the Bible reported them as doing. The stele of the Egyptian king Merneptah, found near Thebes in 1896, had already had a similar effect on the study of Moses: it showed that there was a people called 'Israel' in Palestine in the thirteenth century BC, just about the time when Moses should have lived if the biblical record was broadly accurate. By 1959, when John Bright wrote his still-classic *History of Israel*, most Anglo-Saxon biblical scholars were convinced that the early history recorded in Genesis and Exodus was not legendary at all, but grounded in genuine memory. German scholarship remained broadly unconvinced. But it too began to be very interested in at least the pre-monarchic age, as we shall now see.

THE BEGINNINGS OF ISRAEL

Nineteenth-century scepticism about the biblical record had generally not extended to the stories of the conquest of Canaan under Joshua. With this period, it was thought, we were on more or less historical territory. However, the German scholars Albrecht Alt (1883–1956) and Martin Noth together challenged this picture, calling forth a strong reaction from the 'biblical archaeologists'.

They suggested that we should speak of a 'settlement' rather than a 'conquest' of the land. The book of Joshua's presentation of a concerted military campaign against Canaan was an exaggeration; what had really happened was something more like a slow infiltration, in which incomers had first settled the hill country of Palestine, and only later moved to take over (rather than destroy) the Canaanite cities. There was indeed little evidence on the ground for the kind of sudden destruction implied in Joshua. Kathleen Kenyon (1906–78), for example, had dug at the site of ancient Jericho, and had found no evidence of the walls that supposedly fell down at Joshua's army's trumpet-blasts (Joshua 6) in any period that could at all plausibly be associated with an Israelite invasion. This argument used the archaeology of Palestine against the 'biblical archaeologists', and in this it was a foretaste of things to come.

For by the late 1950s, even as Bright was writing, the tide was beginning to turn back in a more sceptical direction, and archaeology itself contributed to this. From the 1960s there developed a new approach to the excavation of 'biblical' sites, in which one no longer looked for confirmation or refutation of what the Bible said, but examined sites as one would in any other country to discover what they could tell us, quite independently of any biblical accounts. This soon came to be linked with a quest for information about the inhabitants of a site over long periods, rather than for single cataclysmic events. Large-scale surveys, instead of spot-digs, started to reveal patterns of habitation, and what emerged supported the infiltration theory by showing little evidence of sudden changes of culture, and went beyond that to put in question whether there had indeed been *any* change of population at all in most of the cities mentioned in Joshua and Judges. At the same time the idea arose—partly under Marxist influence—that the early Israelites might have been distinguished from the Canaanites they supposedly replaced by social class rather than ethnicity. N. K. Gottwald and G. E. Mendenhall both developed a theory that the origins of Israel lay in a 'peasants' revolt' against Canaanite overlords, rather than in a conquest *or* an infiltration. Israelites were really Canaanites, but Canaanites with a low social status. This seemed to link plausibly with the long-observed fact that what the Egyptians and others called *habiru* (a word possibly connected with 'Hebrew') were a low social class rather than an ethnic group.

REDATING THE SOURCES

While all this was going on, the antiquity of the patriarchal and Mosaic traditions was also being challenged, and by North Americans. John Van Seters and Thomas L. Thompson argued trenchantly that the evidence from Mari and Nuzi had been mis-interpreted: the customs recorded there did occur in the second millennium, but they persisted until well into the first, so the earlier period was not after all a 'unique congenial context' for the stories of the patriarchs. Furthermore, even the biblical sources dealing with Abraham's family and with Moses were later than the tradi-tional dating. As we have seen, Wellhausen had dated these stories to the pre-exilic period, probably the ninth and eighth centuries BC. He thought that, even if they were that early, they were too late to preserve any genuine memories of the periods they purported to describe. Van Seters and Thompson, together with the German scholar Lothar Perlitt, argued that even Wellhausen had been too optimistic. 'J', the earliest of the Pentateuchal sources, was much later than the eighth century, since it showed acquaintance with the great prophets of that period: Moses, in J, was made in the image of a prophet such as Isaiah. The stories could not be earlier than the late exilic age, that is, the mid-sixth century. J and P did not represent two stages in the development of Israel's thought, but were alternative near-contemporary versions of the story of Israel.

Despite strong opposition from more traditionally-minded readers of the Hebrew Bible, the tendency to date the relevant sources even later than they were dated by such as Wellhausen has continued, and this, linked with the demise of a distinctly 'biblical' archaeology, has produced a situation in which there is once again wholesale scepticism about the accuracy of the biblical story of early Israel. Recently this has extended also to the period of the early monarchy, with the claim that Jerusalem in the days of 'David' (if he ever existed) was a tiny town not at all capable of accom-modating the much-vaunted splendours of Solomon, his supposed successor. Going even further, Thompson, together with N. P. Lemche and P. R. Davies, have argued for yet later datings of biblical materials, claiming that all the stories of the monarchic period originated in the Persian or even the Hellenistic age—thus at last producing agreement between biblical scholars and the general public that the story the Bible tells is a fiction.

As indicated above, I am sceptical of such extreme scepticism. It is hard to believe that the detailed stories in Samuel and Kings were composed out of someone's head, and have no rootage in any historical events at all. Even in the much earlier material, the stories of the patriarchs and Moses, there remains an unexplained residue from the work of the biblical archaeologists. Why are the names in these stories so unlike those in later times; why does Moses, indeed, have a definitely Egyptian name, as do Aaron, Hophni, and Phineas, all characters in the exodus story which is set in Egypt? Can these be simply very late fiction? Are the 'books of the annals of the Kings of Israel and Judah', so liberally referred to in Kings, simply be part of an elaborate fiction? These questions continue to worry the majority of Old Testament scholars, and to suggest that the pendulum may have swung too far. Many still think that there is substantial pre-exilic material in the Hebrew Bible, and that it succeeds in recording some of the major events of that time without undue distortion, so that we really do have some information about the age of the great prophets—from the eighth century down to the exile in the sixth. But it is increasingly recognized that our knowledge of Israel before the eighth century is extremely sketchy, and that the lively stories about David, for example, in 1 and 2 Samuel, owe a great deal to the storyteller's art, even though they are told about a person who almost certainly did exist.

What recent study does justify, however, is a move back to a position something like Wellhausen's. The Old Testament material was not created out of thin air, but nor is most of it history in anything like our sense, and reconstructing an account of Israel's development over time on the basis of it is fraught with much more difficulty than the optimism of a work such as John Bright's *History of Israel* ever recognized. There are sources in the Old Testament that may be quite reliable historically: this may be true of parts of Kings, where we often have Assyrian or Babylonian corroboration in broad outline, and also of the Memoirs of Nehemiah in the book that bears his name (Nehemiah 1–7; 12:27–47; and 13), a precious source for the otherwise very obscure history of the Persian period in Judah (or

'Yehud', as it was known in Aramaic). But from much of the narrative in the Hebrew Bible we learn mainly about the time in which it was written, not about the time it purports to chronicle—just as Wellhausen said, over a hundred years ago.

HISTORY AND THE NEW TESTAMENT

Reconstructing the history of New Testament times is a vastly different task from investigating the history of ancient Israel and Judah, because the available sources are so much closer to the time concerned. In Paul's letters we have documents actually written in the midst of the growth of the Christian churches, and thus contemporary with the events they refer to; and there is relevant evidence in the writings of other contemporary Jewish figures, especially the Jewish historian Flavius Josephus, and of classical writers, particularly Tacitus. The careers of such people as Pontius Pilate can be established from such sources without much room for doubt, and a good deal is known about the political organization of Palestine and the Mediterranean world in the period. The really problematic material is the story of Jesus in the Gospels. By general consent none of these is earlier than the 60s, and many scholars think all of them were composed after the fall of Jerusalem to the Romans in AD 70, in which case they are at least one whole generation removed from any eyewitness memories of the figure of Jesus. The 'quest of the historical Jesus' is thus a major part of the historical work of New Testament scholars, and it cannot be said to have yielded any very secure results except on minimally controversial issues (such as that his mother was called Mary and that he was crucified under the procuratorship of Pilate).

THE ROMAN EMPIRE AND THE NEW TESTAMENT

The setting of New Testament history is well documented. All of the world around the Mediterranean, where Christian missions were active in the days of Paul, and partly through his own journeys, was part of the Roman Empire: Christian missionaries did not venture to outlandish areas such as those north and east of the Rhine until later times. Palestine itself was governed in a most complicated way: people often say it was 'under Roman

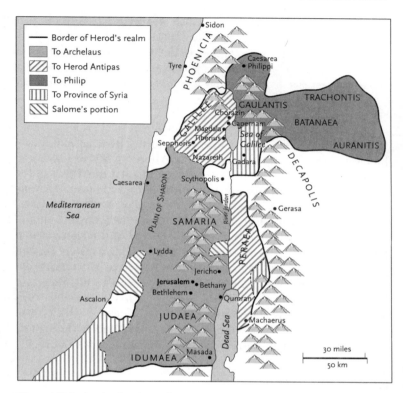

Figure 4 Palestine in the time of Jesus

occupation', but this is an oversimplification. E. P. Sanders sums up the situation as follows:

In Galilee there was no official Roman presence at all. Greek-speaking Gentiles lived in the cities that they had long inhabited, which formed a kind of crescent around Galilee: there were Gentile cities to the east, to the north and to the west. In geographical Galilee there was one Gentile city, Scythopolis, but it was independent of political Galilee. In Judaea [which was officially a Roman province] the official Roman presence was very small. There was one Roman of rank in residence, and he was

> supported by a handful of troops. This Roman and his small military force lived among a lot of other Gentiles in Caesarea, seldom came to Jerusalem, and did nothing to plant Graeco-Roman laws and customs in the Jewish parts of the country. In Jerusalem there was not a substantial Gentile presence ... Effective rule was in the hands of local aristocrats and elders.
>
> (E. P. Sanders, 1993:27)

Palestine mattered to the Romans not for its own sake, but as a buffer between both Egypt and Asia Minor (what we now call Turkey), which were sources of great wealth, and the 'Parthians'— the inhabitants of Mesopotamia. As throughout its history, Palestine occupied a strategic position, and that was why the Romans were interested in it. They had no particular desire to Romanize it and did not mind that it retained its own Jewish culture, provided it posed no political threat—which it mostly didn't. Even though Judaea was a province, it had an 'ethnarch', Herod the Great's son Archelaus (Matthew 2:22), who also ruled Samaria to the north and Idumaea to the south; while the ruler ('tetrarch') of Galilee was another son, Antipas. The territory to the east of the sea of Galilee was ruled by Philip. Jesus and his disciples moved freely through all these areas, as did Paul some years later: the borders were porous.

BEHIND THE NEW TESTAMENT

The detailed problems of reconstructing the history behind the New Testament do not arise from conflicts between the New Testament and other sources, but from discrepancies within the New Testament itself. In general no generic question arises: that is, the intention of most New Testament books that touch on historical matters does appear to be to convey literal historical fact, though some have seen the arrangement of Luke's Gospel plus Acts, for example, as involving 'theological' history, where the facts have been adjusted to serve a theological scheme. Both the Gospels and Acts may include folklore elements, but there seems little doubt that neither is intentional fiction in the way that is sometimes suggested for parts of the Old Testament: deliberate fiction is confined to the parables, which are presented as illustrative stories, not as fact.

But whether the proposed facts of the Gospel narratives really are such is of course another matter, and many readers think that the details of the stories of Jesus' birth and infancy in particular, as also of the resurrection appearances, are embroidery by skilful story-tellers. In these, too, there is the problem of internal discrepancies: though in the popular imagination Jesus' birth involved all the incidents in both Matthew and Luke's versions, as they stand the two Gospels tell different stories—the wise men appear only in Matthew, the shepherds only in Luke. And whereas Matthew assumes that Mary and Joseph lived in Judaea and only went to Nazareth (in Galilee) to escape danger from Archelaus after they returned from fleeing to Egypt, for Luke Nazareth was the home from which they made the journey to Bethlehem for Jesus' birth because of the (purported) census. (John, like Matthew, seems to assume that Judaea was Jesus' home ground.)

Even with Paul, for whom we have both the evidence of the letters and the account in Acts, it is hard to extract a clear chronology and itinerary because these two sources of information appear to conflict. It is possible from Acts to reconstruct a framework into which Paul's letters can be slotted, but there are problems. The largest problem is Paul's assertion in Galatians (2:1) that fourteen years of his ministry unfolded before he went to Jerusalem, which is not at al the impression given in Acts. It suggests that Paul worked far more independently of Jesus' other early followers than the author of Acts allows, and did not go regularly to Jerusalem to check on the 'authenticity' of his message. This and other problems in co-ordinating Acts and the letters in turn call in question how accurate Acts really is. Roman historians have often seen it as very well informed about the detail of Roman government in the provinces, and of that there can be little doubt. But when it comes to the details of Paul's life, there is probably more imaginative reconstruction than the sober style might lead one to suspect.

THE QUEST OF THE HISTORICAL JESUS

But the historical problem in the New Testament that interests most readers is what is usually called the quest of the historical Jesus, from the title of the 1910 translation into English of the famous book by Albert Schweitzer published in 1906 (and originally called

Von Reimarus zu Wrede). That book surveyed work on the historical figure of Jesus from the work of H. S. Reimarus in the late eighteenth century, which set the agenda for the investigation of Jesus' life and work and raised issues that are still current today. Reimarus's work provided, as Schweitzer put it, 'a magnificent overture in which are announced all the motifs of the future historical treatment of the life of Jesus' (1906: 26). He wrote a long work entitled *An Apology or Defence for Rational Worshippers of God*, which remained unpublished at his death in 1768. Parts of it however were published by G. F. Lessing in 1774–78: they consisted of attacks on the historical probability of a number of allegedly historical events in the Bible, including the crossing of the Red Sea by the Israelites, in the interest of establishing, in the place of a religion of miracle, a reasonable, deistic religious system for the 'rational' worshippers of God of his title. But in the final fragment published by Lessing in 1778 he dealt with 'The Intentions of Jesus and his Disciples', and here he applied an equally non-supernaturalistic interpretation to the story of Jesus. First, contrary to the Gospel accounts, he suggested that the disciples had stolen the body of Jesus to give credence to their story that he had been raised from the dead. Second, Reimarus linked this to a reconstruction of the teaching of the disciples in which they had invented one of the major planks of Jesus preaching as presented in the Gospels, that is, its eschatological orientation. The Jesus of the Gospels speaks of the coming 'kingdom of God', but he originally meant by this an imminent earthly restoration of power to Israel. The disciples turned it into a proclamation of a coming cosmic intervention by God in which all human beings would be judged and consigned to heaven or hell.

Both of these theories still have their supporters. Most would agree that Jesus' message, even if originally eschatological in some sense, has been inflated by his followers and turned into an otherworldly hope instead of remaining rooted in historical reality— though some (for example, the members of the 'Jesus Seminar' in the USA) tend to think that his teaching was not eschatological at all. And though the theft of his body is not nowadays the commonest explanation of the resurrection stories, the belief that he was not resurrected in a literally physical sense is widely accepted. But much more important than the details of Reimarus's theses is the fact that they established, for the first time, that the story of Jesus could be analysed and dissected as though it were the record of a historical figure like any other, and to which no special rules applied. It was the beginning of a quest for the *historical* Jesus, without the privileging of Christian belief about him, which could in principle be undertaken by anyone with the necessary historical tools, irrespective of their own faith-commitment.

D. F. STRAUSS

A first major attempt to approach the historical Jesus in a systematically historical way was made by David Friedrich Strauss in his *The Life of Jesus*, published in 1835—a work that became known in Britain through its translation by the novelist George Eliot. For Strauss, the historical Jesus and the 'Christ of faith' belonged in separate boxes, and no amount of historical work could undermine the Christian commitment to the 'eternal truth' of the gospel message (understood by Strauss in accordance with the philosophy of Hegel). But just for that reason the historical investigation could be as hard-hitting as it liked, and in Strauss it was very hard-hitting indeed. The story of Jesus involved any number of legendary elements, which could make no claim to historicity: miracles of healing and of nature (walking on the water, for example, or the Virgin Birth) that were simply incredible to any modern person. And the Gospel accounts were radically incompatible with each other and could not be harmonized, despite all the efforts in that direction that had been made from the early Church onwards. Jesus emerged as, in human terms, nothing much like the Church's picture of 'the Christ'; Christianity as a religion could survive only by transforming itself into a religion of the spirit, that did not depend on the vagaries of history at all, but on spiritual principles quite unconnected to the particularities of life in first-century Palestine.

Reimarus and Strauss together set the agenda for subsequent work on Jesus as a historical figure. This work has not always had the debunking effect that people felt in those pioneers, but it has consistently tried to examine the records of Jesus' life without supernaturalist assumptions about his divine nature, insofar as these would be used to underpin the historicity of recorded events or sayings that on rational grounds must be judged improbable or impossible. Like their Old Testament counterparts, who often tend towards historical credulity where the biblical record is concerned, even though they theoretically approach it as detached historians, New Testament scholars have rarely been neutral in their conclusions about the historical Jesus. Nearly always he has emerged as someone they can continue to reverence, and very often he has been made in the image of their own preferred version of Christianity. This was certainly true of Schweitzer, whose Jesus is a consistently eschatological figure who orchestrated his own death in an attempt to bring in the kingdom of God, and it remains true today. But in principle the aim is to reconstruct a historical figure among other historical figures, not someone who cannot be contained by historical method because he is divine.

THREE QUESTS

There are sometimes said to have been three 'quests' for the historical Jesus. The first is taken to have lasted from Reimarus, through Schweitzer, and up to the work of Rudolf Bultmann (1884–1976). Bultmann maintained, with arguable consistency, that since the Christ of faith did not depend on the Jesus of history (see Strauss), then for theology it was not important what the historical Jesus actually did or said. In his view we had no authentic material about Jesus anyway, only the traditions about him that the early Church had handed down in the Gospels, which rested on repeated retellings of stories whose linkage with real history was always uncertain. For Bultmann the stories of Jesus are very like parables: they have no rootage in actual events, or if they do, we cannot know that they do. Even more than for Strauss, the historical Jesus is really an irrelevance for faith: in Paul's words, 'though once we regarded Christ from a human point of view [Greek: according to the flesh], we regard him thus no longer' (2 Corinthians 5:16). Bultmann's work was thus felt to have put an end to the quest for the historical Jesus. Existential commitment to Jesus, not historical knowledge of him, was what mattered.

In former students of Bultmann, however, interest in this forbidden subject revived, and we find Günther Bornkamm, for example, writing a biography of Jesus! (*Jesus of Nazareth*, London: Hodder & Stoughton, 1963). In the middle years of the twentieth century, inspired by such followers of Bultmann who had recanted on the pure Bultmannian gospel, we do find what James Robinson called a 'new' quest for the historical Jesus (J. M. Robinson, *A New Quest of the Historical Jesus*, London: SCM Press, 1959). It cannot be said, however, that it produced much that was genuinely new, representing on the whole a watering-down of the extreme historical nihilism into which the first quest had ended but to which it was arguably committed in principle.

But the last decades of the twentieth century and the opening decade of the twenty-first have witnessed an explosion of interest in the historical Jesus—the so-called 'third quest'. This has a number of strands. One has been the major rediscovery of the Jewishness of Jesus, in which a major player has been the Jewish (but once Catholic) New Testament scholar, Geza Vermes. Traditionally Jews have not been very interested in Jesus, partly because to show an interest invites suspicion of being a crypto-Christian, but also partly because the Jewish religion simply has no place for Jesus—he does not belong to its structures. He is usually seen by Jews, if he is thought about at all, as simply a heterodox Jew who led some Jewish people astray and was turned into the core of a new and non-Jewish religion by the 'apostle to the Gentiles', Paul. Vermes however resolved to examine Jesus as a historical figure within the matrix of the Judaism of his own day, now illuminated so much by such newly discovered works as the Dead Sea Scrolls. His aim was to show how Jesus fitted into his context, on which Vermes is an acknowledged expert. Jesus emerges as a not untypical Galilean teacher of his time. The combination of wonder-working and wise teaching is not a contradiction, but is a common feature of holy men of the period. Even the disciples' belief in his resurrection, though not closely paralleled elsewhere and (of course) not to be accepted, is quite thinkable in context. Jesus emerges as a less unorthodox figure than Jews have traditionally conceived him as; but from a Christian point of view he is therefore much more Jewish than Christianity has ever realized. This thus represents a fresh challenge for Christian believers, for whom the continuity between Jesus and the (mainly Gentile) Church is thereby called in question.

The Jewishness of Jesus is also a theme in the work of E. P. Sanders. His book *The Historical Figure of Jesus* (London: Allen Lane—the Penguin Press, 1993) is one of the most accessible accounts of what we can know about Jesus as modern historians. Sanders takes for granted that Jesus makes sense against a Jewish background. This indeed is in a way obvious; it needs affirming, however, because so much energy had been expended in the previous quests on the 'principle of dissimilarity', which states that those teachings are to be seen as both historically attributable to and distinctive of Jesus that could not be predicted from contemporary Judaism (or from the beliefs of the later Church). In a way this principle has a clear validity on its negative side. If we find Jesus teaching something that was unprecedented, then that at least is likely to have been a real part of his message, since no one would have invented it. But positively it does nothing to deal with cases where what Jesus teaches *coincides* with the contemporary teachings of Judaism or of early Christians, since these might or might not be genuine. And it is very implausible to think that what Jesus taught was 100 per cent distinctive, since then no one would have been able to understand him at all.

So an overlap with contemporary Judaism, as well as some continuity with later Christianity, is inherently likely, and one would expect what Jesus taught to exhibit both similarity and dissimilarity with other contemporary beliefs: that is true, after all, of any distinctive and creative figure. Perhaps a better criterion is the principle of *plausibility*, as exemplified by Gerd Theissen and Dagmar Winter in their work *The Quest for the Plausible Jesus* (London: SCM Press, 2002): those teachings and actions attributed to Jesus that make sense in their historical and intellectual context are likely to go back to him. On some such basis it may be possible to reconstruct him as a historical figure without taking him out of his context, yet to do justice to the fact that there was clearly something unusual and distinctive about him—or why would so many stories have attached themselves to him? One of the problems in seeing Jesus as simply a typical teacher of his time is to explain why then he was crucified: he must have said or done *some* things that were regarded as outrageous.

THE TEACHING OF JESUS

Apart from the discussions by Vermes, two positions have established themselves on the question of Jesus' teaching. One continues in the tradition of Schweitzer and emphasizes the eschatological element. This is true of Sanders, who shows that Jesus must have been prophesying an overthrow in the current order of things, or else he would never have been arrested and executed. This was not, however, a cosmic change: he thought on the level of the political and social, rather than the metaphysical. Through his own ministry he hoped to inaugurate the kingdom of God, understood as a new type of relationship between people, and between people and God, based on acceptance of the marginalized. What this might have amounted to in practice can be seen attractively illustrated in Theissen's historical novel *The Shadow of the Galilean: The Quest of the Historical Jesus in Narrative Form* (London: SCM Press, 1982). Jesus' eschatology had very little in the way of condemnation or judgement in it, but it saw the possibility of a society transformed through the love of God.

Such an eschatological perspective on Jesus can also be found, developed in great detail, in the works of N. T. Wright. He seeks to show that Jesus' role was to initiate the kingdom of God, again understood in earthly terms, but involving such a transformation of society that it really represented the breaking in of a new divine order. In Jesus, the destiny of Israel was finally to be fulfilled, so that he represented 'the climax of the covenant'.

The other position on the teaching of Jesus is represented by the work of the Jesus Seminar in the USA, which meets periodically to vote on the probability that this or that saying in the Gospels really goes back to Jesus himself, using different coloured balls to indicate different degrees of likelihood. Its prominent member, John Dominic Crossan, has argued the case for a non-eschatological Jesus. The controlling idea is of Jesus as a wise man or sage, similar in some ways to the Cynics, who delivered a kind of aphoristic wisdom not unlike that found in Old Testament wisdom literature. The gospel he proclaimed had nothing to do with any cataclysmic historical events, but was focused entirely on how to live a good life, rather as in the teaching of Hellenistic sages in the same period. This fed into the kind of Christian teaching that was eventually deemed heterodox by the Church and condemned as 'gnosticism', in which salvation depended on the believer's knowledge rather than on the death and resurrection of Jesus, which were of marginal importance. Sayings that suggest otherwise are the invention of the 'orthodox' party in the early Church, and do not derive from Jesus himself, who had no kind of eschatological message about a divine plan for the world, whether this- or other-worldly.

So much for the historical Jesus as a teacher. It is clear that both these assessments cannot be right, and it seems to me that Sanders and Wright are probably correct in thinking that one cannot easily eliminate all the eschatological material from Jesus' teaching. Above all, there needs to be something to explain why he became so unpopular with the authorities, and was eventually tried and executed. It is hard to see why this should have happened to a wisdom teacher; much easier to understand it if he was preaching a message that could at least be heard as predicting the imminent divine overthrow of the existing social order. Sanders plausibly argues that the incident traditionally called the 'cleansing of the Temple' was crucial. In it Jesus did not oppose the use of the Temple as a place of trade—it was essential to the sacrificial system that people could buy animals there for the sacrifices—but used a symbolic act to signal that the Temple would be overthrown, and that with it the existing forms of Jewish society would come to an end. This was politically inflammatory, and it is not surprising that it called forth retribution from both the Jewish and the Roman powers.

MIRACLES

Despite modern rational objections to the idea of miracles, there seems little doubt that his contemporaries believed Jesus could work wonders, especially of healing, and the miracle-stories are thus an integral part of the Gospel-record. Other near-contemporary Galileans, Onias the Circle-Drawer and Haninah ben Dosa, were noted wonder-workers, and they are discussed at length by Vermes. The attempt to reduce the 'non-rational' aspect of Jesus' life cannot succeed without taking him outside the culture in which he made sense. He was clearly remembered as 'a prophet great *in deed and word*' (Luke 24:19, my emphasis) by later generations, and it is highly probable that both strands were genuinely present in his life and work. Historical study of the figure of Jesus since Reimarus has resisted tearing him from his historical environment, and this is almost certain to mean recognizing in him features that would be strange in a modern figure, including a reputation as a healer and a message that made sense against the background of its time—just as the prediction of imminent divine intervention certainly does, since it is known that there was a good deal of eschatological expectation in this period.

SOURCES FOR JESUS

Most discussions of the historical Jesus in recent times concentrate on the three Synoptic Gospels, Matthew, Mark, and Luke. It is widely held that the Gospel of John is both markedly later—probably from not long before the end of the first century—and represents a reworking of tradition about Jesus in the interest of a particular theology (which is not to say that the Synoptics do not have distinctive theological slants too, as 'redaction critics' have long recognized). There have been critics who believed there was substantial historically accurate material in John—C. H. Dodd was a particularly distinguished representative of this view; but most scholars think it has been so restructured that we learn little of importance for the quest of the historical Jesus from this Gospel. We may be able to learn a lot about the theological beliefs of the community that produced its author/compiler: that is another matter.

THE INFANCY AND RESURRECTION STORIES

What of the beginning and end of the story of Jesus? All three quests tend to be light on discussion of the stories of Jesus' birth and infancy. For most biblical critics, this material is seen as more or less legendary, and as having value in symbols and imagery but not as a historical source. This is one of the ways in which biblical scholarship diverges most radically from popular religious belief. In Matthew, and even more in Luke, the nativity stories are written in a distinctive biblical style, reminiscent of the Greek translation of the Hebrew Bible, and this helps to establish an atmosphere that sets them apart from the story of Jesus' adult life. He is presented as resembling Moses or Samson in being marked out by a divinely announced birth, and it is in these stories and nowhere else in the New Testament that we are told that his mother was a virgin. The stories are also akin to some Hellenistic biographies of heroes. Though it is possible to imagine means by which the stories could have passed down to the evangelists, most scholars treat them as works of fiction designed to glorify the figure of Jesus.

The resurrection is in rather a different category. The stories of the appearances of the risen Jesus are no more consistent with each other than are the Matthaean and Lukan nativity and infancy stories, but there is the crucial difference that the resurrection of Jesus and the fact that he appeared to various disciples is attested by Paul, at a much earlier date than any of the Gospels. Paul's account, in 1 Corinthians 15:3–11, has not been assimilated to the stories in the Gospels, since it is at odds with them in identifying not the women at the tomb but Peter as the first witness of the resurrection, and in asserting that the risen Lord appeared to a large number of disciples ('five hundred brethren at one time'). There seems no doubt that something odd and unexpected happened after Jesus' crucifixion and burial, though the biblical critic is not in a position to tell what it was. As Sanders puts it: 'That Jesus' followers (and later Paul) had resurrection experiences is, in my judgement, a fact. What the reality was that gave rise to the experiences I do not know' (*The Historical Figure of Jesus*, 1993:280).

FURTHER READING

For the history of Israel, a good basic text book is J. H. Hayes and J. M. Miller, *Israelite and Judaean History*, Philadelphia: Trinity Press International, 1977, read together with Miller's discussion of theoretical issues in his *The Old Testament and the Historian*, London: SPCK, 1976. But things have moved on very much in the last thirty years, and it is important also to read an account of modern developments, such as H. G. M. Williamson (ed.), *Understanding the History of Ancient Israel*, Oxford: Oxford University Press for the British Academy, 2007, or L. L. Grabbe, *Ancient Israel: What do we Know and How do we Know it?* London: T & T Clark, 2007. For history after the exile an excellent guide is provided by Grabbe's *Judaism from Cyrus to Hadrian*, Minneapolis: Fortress, 1992, and *A History of Jews and Judaism in the Second Temple Period*, London: T & T Clark, 2004.

For the history of the New Testament period, L. L. Grabbe is again a reliable guide, in his *An Introduction to First Century Judaism: Jewish Religion and History in the Second Temple Period*, London: T & T Clark, 2004. See also Sarah Pearce, 'Judaea under Roman Rule, 63 BC–135 CE', in John Barton (ed.), *The Biblical World*, London: Routledge, 2002 and Martin Goodman, *Rome and Jerusalem: The Clash of Ancient Civilizations*, London: Allen Lane, 2007.

There is an enormous literature on the historical Jesus, and a pathway through it is offered by E. P. Sanders, *The Historical Figure of Jesus*, London: Allen Lane—the Penguin Press, 1993. The highly significant contribution of Geza Vermes can be sampled in his *Jesus the Jew: A Historian's Reading of the Gospels*, London: SCM Press 2001 (sixth edition). On the earlier 'quests' see Robert Morgan, 'Jesus', in John Barton (ed.), *The Biblical World*, London: Routledge, 2002; M. Borg, *Jesus in Contemporary Scholarship*, Valley Forge, Pa.: Trinity Press International, 1994. For recent developments see Gerd Theissen and Dagmar Winter, *The Quest for the Plausible Jesus*, London: SCM Press, 2002.

6

THE SOCIAL WORLD OF
THE BIBLE

The books of the Bible did not come down from heaven, but were compiled and written by real people in particular social and historical circumstances. The last chapter examined what we can know of the history behind the Bible, but now we consider the variety of social contexts in ancient Israel, early Judaism, and the beginnings of the Christian church that provided the background for the creation of what would eventually become Scripture.

PRE-EXILIC ISRAEL

How far back can we go in the story of Israel if we are looking for a real social context within which the books of the Hebrew Bible began to be written? Many people assume that the Bible had its origin among nomadic desert tribes who had not yet settled in the Promised Land, and consequently that it is marked by concerns proper to a kind of Bedouin culture. The austere, single God worshipped by the Israelites is seen as typical of the life of such wandering groups, who did not yet have the kind of settled and cultivated existence in which the plurality of gods we hear about in the Hebrew Bible belonged. Israel's religion was a simple religion of the desert, and only after the settlement in the land did it become corrupted through contact with Canaanite religion.

This is something like the picture the Hebrew Bible itself paints, but as we saw in the previous chapter its historical foundation is very shaky indeed. There are literally no texts in the Hebrew Bible that plausibly go back into a pre-settlement period. To take one example: the Ten Commandments, though attributed to a revelation to Moses on Mount Sinai, presuppose a settled agrarian community with houses, slaves, and domesticated animals. The oldest texts in the Bible are generally reckoned by scholars to be a few poems. One of them, the Song of Deborah in Judges 5, refers to a conflict in the north of the land not long before the rise of the monarchy in the tenth century BC—long after the putative date of the exodus (thirteenth century). The consensus in modern scholarship is that almost none of the biblical books goes back before the time of the kings, and the tendency in recent times has been to see the eighth century, the time of King Hezekiah and the great prophets Amos, Isaiah, Micah, and Hosea, as the real beginning for Hebrew literature. The literature of the Hebrew Bible reflects a settled, urban society; and its unique single God is the result of a thinning out of the Canaanite gods rather than a pre-existing belief system which those gods threatened. Israelite religion was not a religion of the desert, but of the settled land, and it was formed and transmitted by prophets and scribes, not by tent-dwelling wanderers.

SCRIBES

In the time of the Hebrew monarchies, which is when the Hebrew Bible began to take shape, the structure of society makes it possible to suggest various groups who could have been the source of the books. The Judaean court in Jerusalem, and presumably also the court of the northern kingdom in Samaria, employed a civil service, containing diplomats and others who could communicate with their counterparts in the other Hebrew kingdom and with officials in the civil service of other small countries (Edom, Moab, Ammon, Syria) and of the major powers, Assyria and Egypt. These people, who must have commanded other languages than Hebrew (at least Aramaic and Akkadian), will have been 'scribes'. In the ancient world this does not mean, as we might put it, 'copy-typists', but Secretaries in the sense that term has in our own civil service: people whose learning and familiarity with court protocol and foreign policy made them effective royal servants.

For such scribes to have existed there must have been a system of education, even though we never read of it explicitly in the Hebrew Bible. All of the ancient Hebrew literature that has come down to us must, obviously, have come from literate people, and if any of it is pre-exilic, as most scholars continue to believe, then the scribes of the courts in Jerusalem and Samaria are the likeliest sources for it. It is almost certainly to them that we owe the wisdom literature, since we know for a fact that Mesopotamian and Egyptian wisdom comes from trained scribes who worked in the civil service: Egyptian wisdom books are usually attributed to a royal official, and even if this is a literary fiction it must have been plausible.

What we do not know is how far outside court circles literacy extended. It may be that people acquired the skills of reading and writing at a more elementary level in the home, or by apprenticeship to a local scribe, and it is possible that there were literate people in ancient Israel who were not professional scribes. In this connection it is often pointed out that learning to read and write Hebrew, with an alphabet of just twenty-two characters, is no great achievement as compared with becoming literate in Akkadian with its hundreds of characters, or in Egyptian hieroglyphs.

There is an obscure passage in Isaiah 28:9–13 which seems to refer to children reciting the alphabet, and we possess one early text from Palestine, the 'Gezer calendar', which looks as if it comes from a non-professional writer: it is a mnemonic about the seasons of the year, analogous to our 'Thirty days hath September'. So maybe not all who could write were scribes (Hebrew *sopherim*) in the technical sense. This might explain how we come to have prophetic books from this early period: either the prophets themselves, or some of their disciples, may have been able to write down their oracles. Jeremiah, we learn from Jeremiah 36, had a secretary called Baruch who took down his words when he wanted to preserve them and give them to the king; perhaps other prophets had secretaries too. We have to be on our guard against thinking of the prophets as uncouth figures striding in from the desert, just as we have to revise our picture of early Israel as a nomadic group: the prophets were people who could make skilful use of all the literary resources of ancient Hebrew, and must have been educated people. Amos produced parodies of such diverse forms as the dirge or funeral lament (Amos 5:2), the priestly instruction (4:45) and the wisdom saying (3:3–6).

PROPHETS

The origins of prophecy in Israel are fairly obscure, but this was an institution that existed in many of the cultures of the ancient Near East. In Mesopotamian texts we read of prophets who spoke to kings and gave encouragement or warning when they were consulted (or sometimes spontaneously) in times of political crisis, and their oracles were often recorded in writing. Interestingly one non-Israelite prophet, Balaam (Num. 22–24) appears also in some wall-inscriptions from Deir Allah in Jordan, and so was perhaps a well-known figure of legend throughout the region. The prophets of Israel appear to have been very much the same kind of people. Some of them were solitary, as Elijah seems to have been, while others lived in community, as did the group with which Elisha was associated (see 2 Kings 2:19–22). The prophets of the Hebrew Bible however have two particular characteristics that make them unusual in the ancient world.

First, the 'classical' prophets of Israel (i.e. those who have a book named after them) seem in most cases not to have been professional prophets. They 'prophesy', for there is nothing else one can call their speeches, but they are not 'prophets' in the usual sense. The book of Amos makes the contrast explicit in a little scene involving Amos and the priest of Bethel, Amaziah, who assumes that he has jurisdiction over Amos, as presumably therefore priests did over the prophets who worked at the shrines they served (Amos 7:14–15). But Amos, as presented here, vehemently denies that he is a prophet—and therefore denies that Amaziah can give him orders. He certainly 'prophesies', but he is not a prophet. Rather, he is someone with an ordinary secular occupation, whom God has specially commissioned to deliver an unwelcome message to the people of Israel. There has been speculation about the occupations of the other classical prophets. Isaiah, many think, was a courtier, possibly a court scribe; Ezekiel we know to have been a priest, and Jeremiah came from a priestly family; Hosea too may have had priestly connections. With the other classical prophets we are in the dark; but in the pre-exilic period they do seem to have come from a non-prophetic background.

Secondly, the main message of the pre-exilic prophets is one of impending disaster for the whole nation. Prophets in Mesopotamia often told the king that he should not fight a particular battle because he would lose it if he did. But they never predict the downfall of the nation as a whole, and they do not say that this is because of national sin. This is one of the new notes in the prophecies of Amos. There is discussion about the extent to which the prophets saw restoration beyond judgement. As they stand all the major prophetic books include oracles of blessing, but nearly always they work on the presupposition that disaster will strike first—that is, very few oracles say that disaster will simply be averted. At best we find a message of conditional blessing: 'If you are willing and obedient you shall eat the good of the land' (Isaiah 1:19), but nearly always linked with the possibility of doom: 'but if you refuse and rebel, you will be devoured by the sword' (1:20). And the oracles of blessing may in many cases be post-exilic insertions into the prophets' original words, placed there, once there had been a measure of restoration after the disaster of the Exile, to make the pre-exilic prophets foretell what had in fact happened.

In these ways therefore the classical prophets represent a phenomenon not exactly paralleled in the rest of the ancient Near East. This makes it unlikely that their books are simply post-exilic forgeries: they have distinctive characteristics that a later period would not have invented. Just how numerous they were, and how much impact they had on Israelite and Judaean society, we do not know. Certainly we read of the kings of Judah consulting Isaiah (Isaiah 37) and Jeremiah (Jeremiah 38) in times of crisis. There are stories from an earlier period in which Samuel, also a priest as well as a prophet, is consulted by Saul (1 Samuel 9), but this, like the stories of Elijah and Elisha, may have much of the folktale about it, and is not a secure basis for historical claims. But prophets, both the conventional kind and the unusual figures such as Amos and Isaiah, were certainly part of the social fabric under the kings.

PRIESTS

Amaziah's words to Amos imply that priests normally had jurisdiction over prophets, and there is little doubt that the priesthood did enjoy considerable power and prestige in pre-exilic society.

In general in this period priests were not essential for worship. Whatever may have been the practice in the temple at Jerusalem, at local sanctuaries (*bamoth*, 'high places') the head of a family was the normal person to offer sacrifice on behalf of his family. Priests seem in this period mainly to have had a teaching role, instructing people in the right religious practices rather than officiating themselves. Among the priests the group known as Levites seem to have had a pre-eminent place, judging by the strange story of Micah in Judges 17–18. The man called Micah, supposed to have lived in the days before the monarchy, sets up a shrine, as he is perfectly entitled to do, and is glad when the chance comes to install a wandering 'Levite' as its priest. Clearly he did not need to have a priest, and if he wanted one, that priest need not have been a Levite, but he thinks that 'the LORD will prosper me, because I have a Levite as priest' (Judges 17:13).

Just who the Levites were is unknown. There is a tribe called Levi in the various tribal lists in the Hebrew Bible, but it does not necessarily follow that all Levites were in fact members of that tribe: one gets the impression that the editors of the Hebrew Bible themselves did not know how the tribe and the priests were related. What is clear is that priests enjoyed high prestige in Israel. Whether they wrote anything is unclear, but someone must have codified the laws we find in the earliest collection (Exodus 21–23, the 'book of the covenant'), and since priests were clearly involved in legal administration, they may have been its authors and guardians. When we read that some difficult cases need to be resolved 'before God' (Exodus 22:9), that perhaps means that they were taken to the local sanctuary and heard by the priest(s) there.

'DEUTERONOMISTS'

We have assumed that much of the narrative material in the 'historical' books has a pre-exilic origin, and it may be asked which social group in Israel will have been responsible for it. Again scribes seem likely candidates, but we do not know whether the narratives they produced had a quasi-official status or were a piece of private enterprise. The 'final edition' of the historical books, as noted earlier, is in a style reminiscent of the book of Deuteronomy, and the compilers are therefore often referred to as 'deuteronomists'. People with the same concerns evidently also edited the books of the prophets. But who were the deuteronomists? Presumably they too were scribes, but much more than that we cannot say. It is unclear how they were related (if they were) to the scribes who produced wisdom books such as Proverbs, with its rather more 'secular' flavour. We are really in the dark. This reminds us that we also do not know who the hypothetical author 'J' was: presumably also some kind of scribe. He or she was certainly familiar with myths widespread across the ancient world, judging by the material in Genesis, yet was highly creative in moulding these to form a coherent and consecutive narrative, which no-one so far as we know had ever attempted before. Compiling the Deuteronomistic History is a task on a similarly grand scale, evidently accomplished during the years of the exile, either in Babylonia or, more probably, at Mizpah north of Jerusalem, where the remains of the pre-exilic administration had its base during those years. Perhaps the kind of archivists who had in earlier times recorded simply the salient events of each king's reign became much more creative during this period and began to construct continuous narrative out of some earlier written texts and a lot of oral tradition; but we have tantalizingly few hints as to who they really were.

OTHER GROUPS

Priests, prophets, and 'wise men' or scribes: we know that such groups existed in pre-exilic Israel from the slogan or proverb quoted by Jeremiah in 18:18, 'the law shall not perish from the priest, nor counsel from the wise, nor the word from the prophet'. What other groups were there? Of course there were agricultural workers, potters, artisans of all kinds, shopkeepers, traders (who included women, to judge from Proverbs 31), shepherds, and blacksmiths. The fact that the Hebrew Bible is such a religious document must not make us think that the life of ancient Israel was that of a religious community: far from it. It was in almost all respects a normal ancient society. Religion played a much more central role than it does in modern Europe, but it was never the whole story. But these non-writing occupations leave little trace in the literature. They are, as Sirach was to say, the people who 'keep stable the fabric of the world' (38:24); but we can never get to know them as we can those who leave written records. Hence our account is bound to be skewed, but at least we should realize that it is.

POST-EXILIC YEHUD AND THE DIASPORA

Life for many people in Judah continued through the period of the Babylonian Exile without a break: the exile of the king and his government made little difference to the average farmer. For those who were exiled, of course, the difference was huge. In the 530s a certain number of the exiles returned to Judah, now known as the province of Yehud by the Persian administration, and began to pick up the pieces of their former lives. No doubt during the time when the leaders were in exile the administration, which had moved to Mizpah, continued to have scribes (the country still needed a civil service), prophets, and priests, though we do not know whether any kind of sacrificial worship continued, either in the ruins of the temple or in the nearby shrine at Bethel: perhaps it did.

ELDERS

For the exiled community in Babylon our only evidence comes from Ezekiel, who tells us that the 'elders' of the community used to meet at his house, but does not give us much information beyond that. There may have been worship at the riverside, as that is where Ezekiel received his first vision—Acts, from a much later period, shows that worship at rivers was a custom that Paul and his companions expected to find (Acts 16:13). The elders do seem to have emerged in this period as a central feature of the community's polity, and later we find references to the 'heads of fathers' houses' (Ezra 8:1).

GOVERNOR AND HIGH PRIEST

Once the community in Yehud established itself in the land again, there were some changes in its organization. There was now no king, only a governor (*pechah*) appointed by the Persians, though apparently one with royal ancestry (Zerubbabel). Under him were the heads of houses, but alongside him was the high priest (Jeshua), who seems to have had a major role in government rather than being restricted to 'religious' duties. Some have spoken of a diarchy, rule by two equal officials, rather like the rule by two consuls in the Roman republic. Very soon Zerubbabel disappears from the biblical record, and we do not know what became of him. But subsequent governors may have acquired more powers: the *pechah* is certainly the main figure to be reckoned with in Malachi (1:8). In the next century Nehemiah is an outstanding governor, who seems to have authority, granted by the Persians, that exceeds that of the temple priesthood. Yet in time the high priest would take over civil governance as well as religious leadership, as Yehud changed into a hierocracy. There were kings again for a short period in the second century, in the aftermath of the Maccabean revolt against Hellenistic rule, but on the whole the post-exilic community accustomed itself to having a priest at its head. The high-priestly robes as described in Exodus 39 may well be modelled on those of the pre-exilic king, symbolizing the transfer of power from royal to priestly figures.

In any case the post-exilic period is one in which priestly ideas developed strongly, and the priesthood became much more important than it had been before the exile. It is to this period that we owe the elaboration of the priestly strand in the Pentateuch (P), and the final compilers of the Pentateuch show priestly concerns. The books of Chronicles retell the history of Israel from a wholly priestly perspective, turning David from a warrior into a priest, as Julius Wellhausen tartly observed:

> See what Chronicles has made out of David! The founder of the kingdom has become the founder of the temple and the public worship, the king and hero at the head of his companions in arms has become the singer and master of ceremonies at the head of a swarm of priests and Levites; his clearly cut figure has become a feeble holy picture, seen through a cloud of incense.
>
> (Julius Wellhausen, *Prolegomena to the History of Israel*, 1878:282)

The sacrificial system, which in pre-exilic times had been relatively haphazard and informal, was now tightened up and organized, and since sacrifice might be offered only at the Jerusalem temple, the priests had it firmly under their control. The Levites, who in pre-exilic times had been people eminently qualified for priesthood, turned into a kind of junior clergy, assisting the priests but not offering sacrifice themselves, and among the priests various class-distinctions arose, according to the ancestry each priest could claim. The development can be plotted in the book of Ezekiel and in Chronicles as well as in the priestly parts of the Pentateuch. The priesthood seems to have taken over the scribal roles that were exercised in pre-exilic times by secular scribes: hence the priestly stamp on so much post-exilic literature.

PROPHETS AFTER THE EXILE

Prophecy, however, continued. The post-exilic prophets from whom we have named books seem to fall now into the category that Amos had despised or at least dissociated himself from, that of temple-prophets, more like the standard ancient Near Eastern model than the pre-exilic classical prophets had been. Haggai and Zechariah, in the first generation after the return, concern themselves about the importance of rebuilding the temple: one can imagine what Amos would have said about that! Somewhat later Malachi criticizes those who bring blemished offerings, and after him Joel laments the fact that a plague of locusts have left the country so barren that there are no animals or grain to offer in sacrifice. Prophecy has thus become an adjunct to the priestly leadership, and no longer challenges it. Yehud was not a purely temple state, as sometimes alleged; but the temple and its priesthood were far more central and important than they had been in earlier times. The temple must have had people composing psalms, but we do not know if they were priests or laymen; certainly much of the Psalter must come from this period, even if some psalms are pre-exilic, and it is some time in the post-exilic age that the Psalter was edited and arranged.

JEWS IN BABYLONIA

Back in Babylonia there were many Jews who had decided not to return to their ancestral land, but to stay in the new country. From a cuneiform tablet we know of a family in the fifth century who acted as bankers, the Murashu family. Indeed, from the sixth century onwards there was always a Jewish community in

Mesopotamia, which integrated more or less with the surrounding society, and some of whose members prospered. The Babylonian Jewish community was to become central to Judaism in times long after the Bible, as the community that produced the great monument of Jewish law and practice, the Babylonian Talmud. There was also a significant Jewish community in Egypt, centred on the small military base on Elephantine island near where the Aswan dam now stands, and from them we have a collection of papyri in Aramaic, which shows that they had similar structures to the community in Yehud, though their religious practice may not have been orthodox by Judaean standards, probably involving the worship of a consort for Yahweh. But they were in regular communication with the authorities of the Jerusalem temple, who appear to have raised no queries about this—or indeed about their very existence, even though according to Deuteronomy there was meant to be only one Jewish temple. It looks as though practice and theory were not necessarily the same, as they so seldom are.

THE HELLENISTIC AGE

When we enter the Hellenistic age that followed the death of Alexander the Great (323 BC) we find that various changes have come upon the Jewish community in Israel. By now the high priest was unequivocally the ruler, and Yehud was organized as a hierocracy, though other people than the priests took an active role in leadership, as would be expected. There is a lot to be learned from Sirach, composed in the second century BC, about the role of the 'wise man' (38:24–39). Such people seem to have been employed as ambassadors and administrators, much as they had been under the monarchy, and they ran schools: Sirach 51:23–30 is our first explicit reference to a school, though such institutions must have existed long before this.

During the Hellenistic period, however, a big change came to Yehud because of the activities of the king Antiochus Epiphanes, from his power base in Syria. During his persecution of the Jews there developed two distinct resistance groups among the Jews. One consisted of freedom fighters, the Maccabee family and its supporters; and once they had defeated Antiochus and rededicated the temple, which he had profaned, they began to rule as kings, forming what is known as the Hasmonean dynasty. Thus Israel for a time was once again governed by kings, though the high priest remained centrally important.

The other group was a religious sect who believed that Israel should trust in God and not in military might, and who refused to fight on the sabbath, and this group is usually referred to as the *hasidim* or 'faithful ones'—not to be confused with the Hasidic Jews of more modern times. It is probably from this group that the book of Daniel comes, with its disparaging reference to the Maccabees as a 'little help' (Daniel 11:34) and its encouragement of a passive, quietistic attitude towards the power of Antiochus. We begin to see here the existence of different groups among the Jews distinguished not by social role (wise men, priests, prophets) but by attitude and lifestyle. There continued of course to be priests, administrators, and indeed prophets—the author of Daniel, traditionally referred to as an 'apocalyptist', was the kind of prophet that existed in this period. But Judaism was beginning to develop sectarian distinctions too, and these were to be increasingly important in the first century BC and the first century AD, and hence in the time when the New Testament was being produced by one particular Jewish sect, the Christians.

THE PERIOD OF THE NEW TESTAMENT

In the first century AD the Jews of Palestine were under Roman control, though how direct this was varied in different parts of the country (as discussed in the previous chapter). Certainly in Jerusalem the high priest ruled at the pleasure of the Roman governor, as we see from the Gospels. Jews could not, for example, have any kind of foreign policy of their own, or determine how Roman law was administered. But the Romans, rather like the Persians before them, on the whole allowed local custom and practice to be followed in matters that did not affect their own prerogative. The Gospels are probably right to say that Jewish courts had no power to impose the death penalty, but they were certainly able to rule on matters of religious practice and to administer lesser penalties, such as corporal punishment and fines.

PRIESTS, SCRIBES, AND PHARISEES

In interpreting Jewish law there were several groups of specialists, whom the majority of the people regarded as authentic and worthy of respect. The first consisted of the priests, who ran the temple in Jerusalem but also gave rulings and advice on matters of practice: who owed taxes to the temple, or what could or could not be done legitimately on the sabbath. Together with their assistants, the Levites, priests are said by the Jewish historian Josephus to have numbered 20,000 in this period, a far larger group than one might have expected. But we have to remember that they were not full-time employees of the temple, but people with normal jobs who served in the temple for so many days a year.

The second was a group known as the 'scribes', the heirs of the 'wise men' and 'scribes' of earlier times: laymen who were learned in the *torah* and responsible for copying it and checking fresh copies. They are mentioned a good deal in the New Testament, but exactly who they were remains rather obscure, and we do not know how far they overlapped in function with local 'writers', the kind of people who for a fee would copy a letter for you.

The third was the Pharisees. There is dispute about the origins of the Pharisees, but most scholars think they were the descendants of the *hasidim* of the Maccabean period. Pharisees were not all priests, though priests might be Pharisees; what was determinative was their lifestyle. They were Jews who strove to live all the time in the same state of purity as priests serving in the temple: to take their observance of the *torah* with the same measure of seriousness as a priest had to do when on duty. The nearest (fairly) modern parallel might be the early Methodists, members of the Church of England, both ordained and lay, who sought to live a 'methodical' life, with a rule of prayer and spiritual practice and very high moral standards. Such were also the Pharisees. One might move in and out of the Pharisaic movement; Paul evidently belonged to it before his conversion to Christianity. Josephus tells us there were only six thousand Pharisees in his day, and they were thus a fairly exclusive but widely respected group. Some of Jesus' interpretations of the law in a more rigorous direction, in the Sermon on the Mount, bear some resemblance to Pharisaic thinking, for all that the Gospels portray the Pharisees as his opponents.

SADDUCEES AND QUMRAN COVENANTERS

Two other groups should be mentioned. One is the Sadducees, whom we meet occasionally in the New Testament. Most of them were apparently priests, but not all priests belonged, and it seems as though social standing was a factor: most Sadducees were aristocrats, descendants of past high priests.

The other group was the sectarian community that produced many of the Dead Sea Scrolls, whose power base was in the Judaean desert at Qumran, but which had supporters in Jerusalem too. The Dead Sea community certainly included a group of male celibates, an unusual phenomenon in Judaism, which generally stressed procreation and family life. But there were almost certainly other members who were married. The Dead Sea Scrolls fall in general outside the scope of this volume, except that some of them are our earliest copies of biblical books—several scrolls of Isaiah, for example. Like the Pharisees, the Qumran community was con- cerned with maintaining a higher standard of purity than was usual among Jews at large, and certainly the celibate members lived a life not unlike that of later Christian monks, with the activities of each day highly regulated, and frequent ablutions to restore ritual purity.

John the Baptist, as described in the Gospels, seems a little like a Qumran sectarian, with his austere life lived mostly in the desert, though there is nothing that clearly connects him with the com- munity. The Qumran sect is probably the same as the group described by Josephus as the Essenes.

The community at Qumran were the only 'party' in Judaism that systematically excluded everyone else, regarding themselves as the sole members of the covenant with Israel. Otherwise, except for the priesthood, which was hereditary, people could move from one group to another, and many Jews belonged to none of the groups— just as in earlier times only a few people were prophets, priests, or wise men. What was new in this period, however, was the seriousness with which even 'ordinary' Jews took their religious obligations— pagan writers often pointed it out, whether with respect or derision— and therefore held most of the groups just described in esteem.

JEWISH PARTIES AND THE HEBREW BIBLE

Do we owe any part of our Bible to these groups? Almost all the Hebrew Bible was certainly finished before the Maccabean age, that is, by the end of the second century BC, and most parts are considerably earlier than this: Daniel, the latest book, was probably written in the 160s BC. (We can tell this because one of the apocalyptic visions in the book tells the history of Israel in code, and with great accuracy until 167 BC, after which it does not tally with what actually happened, so we can see that it is at that point that it becomes genuinely 'prophetic' rather than ascribing its pseudo-prophecies to Daniel, who is supposed to have lived in the sixth century.) Qoheleth (Ecclesiastes) is probably from the third century BC, as may be also the Song of Songs. Sirach comes from the second century, and is the first to refer to the Scriptures as a collection, mentioning 'the law and the prophets' as well as other writings (Sirach Prologue).

The only works to come clearly from as late as 100 BC and onwards into the New Testament period are the works of the Qumran community, which they but not other Jews probably regarded as authoritative: such works as the Community Rule, the War Scroll, and the Temple Scroll, the latter of which updates and improves on the consistency of the Pentateuchal ritual legislation. As we have seen, the community also copied scrolls of earlier biblical books, which confirms that most of what is now in the Hebrew Bible was 'canonical' by then. Other groups, particularly the Pharisees, began to develop complex chains of reasoning about the provisions of the *torah*, and in the next few generations, after the destruction of the temple in AD 70, these passed into the rabbinic movement and eventually were written down to form the Mishnah (somewhere in the second century AD) and later still the Talmud, a commentary on the Mishnah.

EARLY CHRISTIANITY

Not much is known about the social structures of the first Christians beyond what can be deduced from the New Testament letters, and the early writers known as the 'Apostolic Fathers', who wrote in the early second century AD. The very first Christians were of course Jews, but if Acts is to be believed a mission to Gentiles developed within the lifetime of the apostles, and was of course promoted vigorously by Paul, whose letters date mostly from as early as the 50s AD. It was not long before the Christian movement had spread into Syria, particularly Damascus and Antioch, and then into what is now Turkey and to various Greek cities such as Corinth. How it then spread further west we do not know, but Paul can write to the Christian community in Rome as a large and thriving one which he had not himself evangelized, so there must have been more missionaries than we hear of in Acts.

CHURCH ORDER

To judge from Paul's letters there does seem to have been a somewhat similar structure in a number of the 'churches', with leaders called by various titles (*episkopos*, which would later become 'bishop'), elder (*presbyteros*), and *diakonos* ('deacon'): it is impossible to say how these offices were related to each other, though by the time of Ignatius of Antioch, half a century and more after Paul, the *episkopos* was the leader of the community, the *diakonoi* were his assistants, and the elders were a kind of church council. To judge from 1 Corinthians 1:16, the first person or family to have been converted and baptized had a special status, too. We also hear of 'widows' as an apparently formal category into which one could be registered, and this is a reminder that part of the appeal of the early Christian movement was its extensive welfare scheme, in which those with low social status or income could be looked after by the community. Acts tells us that there was a dispute in Jerusalem between 'Hebraists' and 'Hellenists' (hard to identify exactly) over how generous was the provision for their respective widows, which would imply that the system arrived very early in the history of the church.

Paul's list of functions within the church, in 1 Corinthians 12, shows how variegated church life was for these early Christians: the church included 'first apostles, second prophets, third teachers, then workers of miracles, then healers, helpers, administrators, speakers in various kinds of tongues' (12:28). It is probably anachronistic to ask which of these were 'formal' ministries and which designate simply the talents particular people displayed. Ministry was fluid and *ad hoc*. What we do see is a great deal of concern on Paul's part

that variety should not turn into anarchy, as he tries to keep together a church that, however new, was already tending to fragment
into parties. In fact, nothing in the New Testament suggests that
the church was ever particularly unified: division and disagreement
marked it from the beginning. Must Christians be Jews or could
Gentiles join? Were prophecy and speaking with tongues more
important, or administration and good governance? What role
could women legitimately play? What difference did Christian
belief make to the relations of masters and slaves? All these questions were answered differently by different people, and there were
few control structures strong enough to constrain anyone to accept
one answer rather than another.

SOCIAL ORIGINS OF CHRISTIAN SCRIPTURE

Where in this welter of activity and discord did the writing of what
was to become Christian Scripture find its place? We possess none
of the original manuscripts (any more than we do for the Hebrew
Bible). But in the case of Paul, and by implication the other letter-
writers, the process is reasonably clear. People who wrote letters in
the Graeco-Roman world usually employed a professional scribe,
and Paul was no exception: once we are given the scribe's name
(Tertius, see Romans 16:22). Paul also seems to have signed the
letters in his own hand (1 Corinthians 16:21, Colossians 4:18; 2
Thessalonians 3:17). The scribe could have been someone who
worked for a fee, as scribes generally did, but he may have been a
literate member of the church, which is probably the case with
Tertius in Rome since he adds his own greetings. As we saw in an
earlier chapter, the letters of Paul were certainly real letters, not
'scripture', yet like all letters in a culture where writing-materials
and scribes were in short supply they had a formality that modern
letters tend to lack, and would have been stored carefully and
re-read time and again.

The context for the origin of the Gospels is much more obscure.
The general tendency in modern scholarship has been to see the
'evangelists' as people who compiled, ordered, and interpreted
stories and sayings of Jesus that had previously circulated orally,
perhaps as part of the early church's preaching and teaching (see the
comments on form criticism in chapter 7). But we know that all

except Mark had access to earlier Gospels, and Luke tells us explicitly that this was so. What was the social context within which the activity of compiling a Gospel—editing oral tradition and reworking earlier Gospels—took place? If each Gospel is essentially local, we should have to imagine the church in question as having at least one learned scribe who could undertake this difficult task—difficult even in today's circumstances, but very difficult indeed when the only writing material was papyrus and any existing document will have taken the form of a scroll, which needed to be constantly rewound as the scribe selected and copied out this or that short section and changed it to suit his own judgement and, perhaps, his church's theological stance.

It is hard to imagine the earliest churches as including such scribes, yet they must have done so, or we should not have the Gospels we have. If we prefer to think of each Gospel as designed for all Christians, and intended to supersede all earlier Gospels, then we have to imagine a church that had the prestige to impose its own Gospel on other churches, or several scribes each of whom could issue an 'authoritative' version of the story of Jesus. The divided and variegated picture of the early churches makes this a difficult scenario to imagine, yet, again, the four Gospels did in fact become authoritative in this way, and soon enough that by the early second century AD they were being quoted by Christian writers as 'official' documents. There is a mystery here that scholarship has not so far completely disentangled. Who were Mark, Matthew, Luke, and John? We really do not know.

SOCIAL AND RELIGIOUS CUSTOMS

INITIATION RITES

Jews were marked out in the ancient world by certain distinctive customs, and the early Christian communities soon developed some of their own while slowly abandoning those of the parent religion. Jews practised the circumcision of male infants, a custom found among many other peoples, especially in Africa, but regarded by them as having a deep religious significance, and linking them with the great forefather Abraham, who had circumcised both himself and his household (Genesis 17). When the Seleucid king Antiochus

Epiphanes, in the second century BCE, prohibited circumcision, this was rightly regarded as an attack on Judaism as such. Whether new Gentile converts to Christianity needed to be circumcised—that is, to become Jews—before they could be fully fledged Christians, was a matter of severe dispute in the earliest church. Paul's Letter to the Galatians is very largely about this issue, and it is clear from Acts that it was a subject of intense debate in early Christianity (Acts 15). When Paul rejects the idea that Gentiles need to take on the 'works of the law' to become disciples of Christ, the issue of circumcision is certainly one that is uppermost in his mind. He himself tells us (Galatians 2:3) that his Gentile assistant, Titus, was not required to be circumcised, though Acts on the contrary says that Timothy, by contrast, was (Acts 16:3).

FOOD LAWS

With circumcision went the complex system of food and purity regulations that still characterizes observant Jews today. The foundation of these lies in the Pentateuch, especially in Leviticus 11 and Deuteronomy 14, but tradition greatly elaborated them, as can be seen from the later Jewish collections, the Mishnah and the two Talmuds (Babylonian and Palestinian), which come from post-biblical times. (The modern orthodox Jewish system of food laws, known as *kashrut*, derives directly from these codes, and attention to which foods are kosher continues to play a major role in observant Jewish households.) The food laws were also attacked by Antiochus, who is said to have compelled Jews to eat pork, and they seem to lie behind the story in Daniel 1, where the exiled Judaeans at the Babylonian court refuse to eat the foreign king's food and insist on a vegetarian diet—though it is not clear that this is literally required by any known food laws. It perhaps represents a wish to be on the safe side. This principle characterizes much Jewish legislation about social customs: to 'put a hedge around the law', as the Mishnah puts it, that is, to establish customs stricter than the letter of the law which, if observed, will ensure that no breach of the law itself can ever occur. The Sermon on the Mount (Matthew 5–8) represents a rather similar Christian attempt, by intensifying the ethical demands of the religion beyond literal observance.

CHRISTIAN IDENTITY-MARKERS

Christians soon established customs that could serve as their own identity-markers in their contemporary world, marking them off from both Jews and pagans. One central custom was the initiation rite of baptism. We know this was often practised in addition to circumcision for male converts to Judaism, and certainly for women, who could not be circumcised (there is no evidence that female genital mutilation was ever practised by Jews). Regular bathing is required in the Pentateuch for purification after bodily discharges, and it was a characteristic feature of life at Qumran. John the Baptist of course practised it, and the Gospels suggest that Jesus' disciples also adopted it as a sign of discipleship to Jesus. In the Pauline churches it became standard, and Paul can take it for granted that converts to the new faith have not only been baptized but have also absorbed a theory about baptism as a symbolic dying with Christ and being reborn through him:

> Do you not know that all of us who have been baptized into Christ Jesus were baptized into his death? We were buried therefore with him by baptism into death, so that as Christ was raised from the dead by the glory of the Father, we too might walk in newness of life.
>
> (Romans 6:3–4)

THE EUCHARIST

The other major Christian practice is the Eucharist or Lord's Supper, which Paul in 1 Corinthians assumes the Corinthian church is observing—though to his mind they are observing it falsely by making it merely a shared meal at which people eat their own food rather than a corporate religious act (1 Corinthians 1:17–22). The institution of the Eucharist is said in the Gospels, as well as by Paul, to go back to Jesus himself at the Last Supper, and there is little reason to dispute this, though some have seen the Last Supper story as an 'aetiological' legend justifying later Christian practice. Paul's evidence, however, comes from little more than twenty years after the event. The sharing of bread and wine was part of regular Jewish meals, as well as of the great Passover dinner, and scholars have not found it easy to decide whether the Last Supper was formally a Passover meal (*seder*) or not, though it clearly took place in the week of Passover and soon acquired overtones of Jesus as the Passover lamb.

In blessing wine and bread early Christians were not deviating from Jewish practice, but in associating them with the death of Christ they were striking out in a new direction, and the Eucharist soon came to be seen as something quite different from any pre-existing Jewish rite. It was celebrated on the first day of the week (Sunday) rather than on the Jewish sabbath (Saturday), associating it with Jesus' resurrection on that day: this was certainly established by the early second century, but Paul already speaks of the first day of the week as a day for Christians to collect money for the community in Jerusalem (1 Corinthians 16:2), and the vision in Revelation is communicated to John on 'the Lord's day' (Revelation 1:10).

RITUAL STATUS OF THE BIBLE

In both religions the Bible itself, in whatever form exactly it existed, functioned in ritual practice. We know from the New Testament that Jewish synagogues had regular readings from the Hebrew Bible, not only from the Torah or Pentateuch but also from the Prophets (Luke 4:17), though it is not known how early the present division of the Pentateuch into weekly portions was established: it may be that in New Testament times some looser system was in operation. Christians probably took over the reading of Scripture in their own assemblies, together, in due course, with readings from the Gospels and the letters of the apostles. Paul already directs that his own letters are to be read publicly, and indeed that is the only feasible form of 'publication' they could have had. By the time of Justin Martyr (*ca.* 100–165 AD) the first part of the Eucharist regularly contained readings from 'the memoirs of the apostles and the books of the prophets'.

FURTHER READING

Most information about the social structures of ancient Israel have to be dug out of books on the history or the literature, though a crucial guide was provided in the last generation by R. de Vaux, *Ancient Israel: Its Life and Institutions*, London: Darton, Longman & Todd, 1973. For both the pre- and post–exilic periods there is much in L. L. Grabbe, *Priests, Prophets, Diviners, Sages: A Socio-Historical Study of Religious Specialists in Ancient Israel*, Valley Forge, Pa.: Trinity Press International, 1995.

For the social institutions of Judaism at the time of Jesus an invaluable source is E. P. Sanders, *Jesus and Judaism*, London: SCM, 1985 and also his *Paul, the Law, and the Jewish People*, Philadelphia: Fortress Press, 1985. On the evidence of the Dead Sea Scrolls, see George Brooke, 'The Dead Sea Scrolls', in John Barton (ed.), *The Biblical World*, London: Routledge, 2002, and Timothy Lim, *The Dead Sea Scrolls: A Very Short Introduction*, Oxford: Oxford University Press, 2005. For early Christian institutions an excellent guide is Philip Esler, *The First Christians in their Social World: Social-Scientific Approaches to New Testament Interpretation*, London: Routledge, 1994.

A useful website for the social world of the New Testament is http://www. torreys.org.bible/

7

BIBLICAL INTERPRETATION TODAY

In earlier chapters we have encountered trends in the modern study of the Bible. Historical reconstruction of the events and social realities underlying the biblical narrative requires the ability to date the various biblical books; and that in turn throws up the possibility that some of the books are composite, with an origin in the combining of two or more source documents. This is especially true in the Pentateuch (and we surveyed some of the current theories about this) and the Gospels, where the main scholarly consensus favours the idea that there were at least two major sources, Mark and 'Q', together with other traditions peculiar to Matthew ('M') and Luke ('L'). The study of these hypothetical sources is generally known in the English-speaking world as source criticism, though in German-speaking scholarship as *Literarkritik*, which it is misleading to translate as 'literary criticism'. At an even more fundamental level, we need to know what actually appeared in the biblical books at the earliest point we can investigate, by comparing one manuscript with another, and this produces the technique known as textual criticism, discussed in chapter 2.

However, these historical investigations into the origins of the biblical text by no means exhaust how the Bible is or ought to be studied. With more modern texts, and even with those produced in classical antiquity, there can be an advantage in knowing about the author's sources; and we certainly want to make sure we have an accurate edition, not one full of printing mistakes or errors by the editor. But the interpretation of texts goes well beyond these rather technical matters. We also want to know what the texts mean. The second half of the twentieth century saw various movements dedicated to interpreting biblical texts in something like the way other texts are interpreted, in a quest for the meaning.

FORM CRITICISM

One basic question in looking for the meaning of a text is to ask about its social context. When we read a play, we are aware not only of the meaning of its words and sentences, but also of the fact that it is a play. Knowing that activates various kinds of expectation in us. For example, we know that the speeches of the various characters do not necessarily express the author's own views as they would if they were part of a speech uttered by the author himself or herself, but are an expression of how the character who is speaking is conceptualized. Thus it is misleading to say that 'Shakespeare believed we are such stuff as dreams are made on', since that may not be his own belief—it is a belief he attributes to one of his characters. Similarly when a male lyric poet describes and praises a woman, we are alert to the possibility that he is using conventional language, not necessarily opening his heart to us, since there are certain traditional ways of writing lyric poems. All this applies also to the Bible. When we read Paul's letters, we may feel sure that we are hearing his own voice, since a letter is a way of expressing what the writer wants to convey (though even then we need to remember how conventional many ancient letters were). But in a Psalm we do not necessarily encounter the author's voice in the same way: a Psalm is a highly conventional type of composition, often intended for constant reuse by many people over a long period of time, and only partially capturing the actual thoughts of any of them.

THE PSALMS

It was in the study of the Psalms, in fact, that this awareness of the conventions of particular genres of literature first became prominent in biblical studies. We saw in chapter 3 that Sigmund Mowinckel tried to reconstruct the social settings of the Psalms—and hence the conventions within which they were written—in considerable detail. But he was following in the steps of Hermann Gunkel, who had been the first to classify the Psalms into various subgenres and to explore the conventions governing each genre. Gunkel, for example, had distinguished individual from corporate psalms, and laments from hymns of praise, and had suggested that each type must go back to a different setting in Israelite worship. This may sound obvious now, but before Gunkel it had been usual to see all the biblical Psalms as essentially lyric poems expressing the emotions and ideas of individual authors. After Gunkel it became usual to think it terms of various liturgical settings in which each kind of psalm would have been appropriate—ceremonies of fasting and lamentation, celebrations for victory in battle, prayers of people in times of suffering and affliction. With these different settings sharply in focus, the meaning of each Psalm could be far more exactly defined. Gunkel's approach came to be known as form criticism, though one could equally well call it type criticism or genre criticism. It sought to establish the *Sitz im Leben* or concrete social context of given texts. Though trialled on the Psalms, it was also to prove fruitful in studying the law codes—and even in the case of narrative texts it encouraged readers to ask in what contexts narratives had developed and how they had been used, for example in worship, in teaching the young, or in public acknowledgement of guilt. Nowadays any biblical scholar faced with a text begins by asking what kind of text it is and how it may have been used. For example, when the Dead Sea Scrolls began to be interpreted, a first move was to classify them (as hymns, laws, biblical interpretations, etc.) and to ask in what contexts in the life of the Qumran community they may have been used. This is part of the legacy of Gunkel.

THE GOSPELS

Mention of narrative, however, points us ahead to the use made of form criticism by New Testament scholars: the major names here are Rudolf Bultmann and Martin Dibelius (1883–1947). They took the stories in the Gospels and grouped them into categories—for example, miracle stories, which end in the crowd praising Jesus' prowess as a healer or wonder-worker (e.g. Matthew 9:27–34), or pronouncement stories, where an event ends in Jesus pointing a moral (e.g. Matthew 12:1–8). They then sought to reconstruct settings in the early Church in which stories of these kinds would have been told. Miracle stories might have been kerygmatic in use, that is, used in preaching the gospel (or *kerygma*, Greek for proclamation) to those outside the Christian community; while pronouncement stories would belong to the Church's internal didactic functions, used in the context of instructing new Christians or encouraging and exhorting more established ones. There might thus be more than one *Sitz im Leben* for early Christian use of the traditions about Jesus. Even before the traditions were crystallized into the sources of the Gospels, stories and sayings of Jesus circulated in the Christian community in these different contexts.

But form criticism was a two-edged sword in studying the Gospels. On the one hand, it opened up the possibility that we could get back behind even sources such as Q or M to the earliest forms of the traditions about Jesus—back to the very first generations of Christians, contemporaries with Paul. But on the other hand it had a challenging effect on claims that the stories about Jesus reflected historical reality. If a miracle story is always told in a particular conventionalized form, then it becomes impossible to know anything about its historical accuracy—or, worse, it becomes likely that it was developed without any attention to historical reality at all. Any story of a miraculous healing will end with a crowd expressing wonder and praising God: hence in any given miracle story we cannot know whether there really was a crowd, and whether, if there was, they actually uttered the words of praise that the Gospels ascribe to them. Bultmann and Dibelius showed that similar forms of story could be found for pagan holy men of the time. Where a story is highly conventionalized, our confidence in its historical accuracy is necessarily reduced.

NARRATIVE IN THE HEBREW BIBLE

This is equally true of stories in the Hebrew Bible, and there two sides of the matter can be seen. Where Wellhausen and his followers had argued that the stories about the patriarchs were very late, since the earliest source that mentioned them, J, was from no earlier than the ninth century BC, Gunkel was able to show that many of the stories must rest on earlier, pre-literary versions that might well go back to a far earlier period. They were like the folktales of many other nations, not invented by the authors who set them down in writing and compiled them into literary documents, but resting on oral tradition, told and re-told in such settings as corporate worship or corporate storytelling around the camp fire. Attending to their likely original *Sitz im Leben* thus had the effect of challenging Wellhausen's late dating for them.

But on the other hand, this offered no succour to anyone who wanted to argue that the stories reflected actual events. For they were, precisely, folk-tale, not historical narratives. It is as if we had believed that the stories of Robin Hood were invented in the nineteenth century, and someone were then to come along, Gunkel-like, to show us that they must have an earlier origin, perhaps even really in the Middle Ages. But any hope this might give us that therefore Robin Hood really existed would be dashed when such a person went in to show us that the stories are conventional medieval folk-tale, developed for entertaining an audience at a feast, for example. That would leave us just as far away as ever from being able to believe that there was a real Robin Hood who actually did the things narrated about him.

This kind of scepticism can of course go too far. Folk-tales often develop around a core of fact, and quite possibly there *was* a real Robin Hood. Gunkel would have conceded that there might have been a real Abraham, and much more Bultmann would have maintained that there was a real Jesus, since the traditions about him that we have in the Gospels are so much more nearly contemporary than those about Abraham. Yet in the end we do not attain to any clear factual knowledge about Jesus, only about the stories people told of him. For Bultmann this was made more palatable because he argued that our ignorance of the historical Jesus was a blessing in disguise: true faith can never rest on factual knowledge, or it would not be faith, so Christians should actually be glad that they know so little of the historical Jesus! But not so many people have followed Bultmann down this somewhat stony path. As we saw in discussing the historical Jesus, many New Testament scholars are far less sceptical than this about the possibilities of historical knowledge about him. Form criticism need not, perhaps, have quite so mini-malizing an effect. But it is certainly a challenge to any naïve belief that the Bible simply presents historical facts.

REDACTION CRITICISM

On the positive side, what form criticism did was to move biblical studies firmly in the direction of a more literary reading of the biblical texts. It forced attention on to the literary genre of the texts, and that meant that the texts could no longer be seen simply as sources to be mined for facts, but became literary works needing evaluation like any other literary works. Instead of asking simply, Is this text telling the truth or not?, critics began to focus on more sophisticated issues: What context does the text come from? Why is it telling us this rather than that? Who wrote it, and what was their aim in writing it? It was rather like the move that all of us make at some point in our experience of newspapers, when we stop regarding them simply as repositories of neutral information and begin to ask meta-questions about them: What is this journalist's bias? Why did he report on that story rather than another one? What is the political slant of the paper he writes for? Ultimately, perhaps: Why is he telling me such lies? Form criticism represents a certain loss of innocence in our relationship with the Bible, which can never be regained.

And the next move after form criticism took that greater sophis-tication to the next level by asking about the intentions and plans of the people who compiled the older folkloric stories into a finished narrative, the people we refer to as the 'redactors' or editors of the Gospels, the Pentateuch, or the Deuteronomistic History. What is their *Tendenz*, that is, what are they trying to prove, what are their assumptions, their prejudices, their agenda or subtext?

THE GOSPELS

In the study of the Gospels redaction criticism arose in the 1960s, as the next logical step after form criticism. Now we knew what the building blocks of the Gospels had been, perhaps we could detect the intention with which they had been put together, and study the architecture of the resulting building. The idea that each of the

Gospels had its own special style or flavour was not new. At least in the case of John, readers had already realized in ancient times that it presented a markedly different story about Jesus from the three Synoptics, and Clement of Alexandria (in the second half of the third century AD) had referred to it as a 'spiritual' Gospel by comparison with the more earthly quality of the others. But no one had treated the Gospels as if they were something like novels, with the disparate materials put together to tell an individually coloured story. If we were to read them in such a way we should see that their testimonies could not be combined, but each must be read as complete in itself.

It is not an exaggeration to say that this redaction-critical approach had consequences even for the liturgy of the churches. Traditionally the readings for Sundays in all the Christian churches that use a lectionary (a syllabus of readings) had darted around from one Gospel to another, not regarding it as significant which version of a Gospel story was used. But from the 1960s, following the insights of the Second Vatican Council, the Roman Catholic Church began to use a lectionary in which each of the Synoptics was assigned a year, so that on a three-year cycle worshippers would hear the distinctive voices of Matthew, Mark, and Luke. The other churches have gradually fallen in behind this way of reading the Gospels, which is enshrined in the *Revised Common Lectionary*. Without redaction criticism it is unlikely that it would have come about. (The fact that there is no year of John, but John is used in Lent and Eastertide, reflects the sense that John does not provide a connected biography of Jesus in the same way as the Synoptics, but a special kind of truth about Jesus.)

Redaction criticism has the same fictionalizing tendency as form criticism. If we are getting Matthew's Jesus or Luke's Jesus, then we are not getting Jesus himself, but only a version of him. It became common to write on the theology of the evangelists, as in Hans Conzelmann's important *The Theology of St Luke*, London: Faber & Faber, 1969. According to Conzelmann, the geographical structure of Luke's Gospel is arranged to make a theological or symbolic point, as Jesus progresses from Galilee to Jerusalem, and it parallels the spreading of the Church in Acts from Jerusalem to Galilee and then beyond to the rest of the Mediterranean world. Again, this tends to call in question the historical accuracy of both the Gospel and Acts, suggesting that Luke had a scheme in his mind and fitted the pre-existing materials he had inherited or obtained into it: his motivation was not historical accuracy but theological instruction.

NARRATIVE IN THE HEBREW BIBLE

In the case of the Hebrew Bible redaction criticism has been used somewhat patchily. Studies of the intention behind the assembling of Pentateuchal traditions to make J or P go back before the advent of redaction criticism in New Testament studies, and already during the Second World War Martin Noth's great work *The Deuteronomistic History* (Sheffield: JSOT Press, 1981, from the German original of 1943) studied in painstaking detail the way an individual writer (as he saw it) had compiled a complete history of Israel in the Promised Land, from entry to exile, by assembling written and oral sources. This writer, as we saw in chapter 3, wanted to show how the history of Israel reflected persistent national sin and had ended in well-deserved disaster. Noth himself described his work as 'traditio-historical criticism', but nowadays we should certainly call it redaction criticism.

Noth followed this by a similar study of the Chronicler (taken to mean the author of 1 and 2 Chronicles, Ezra, and Nehemiah). Here again there has been a decisive shift. Traditionally Chronicles was regarded as a collection of odds and ends with which Samuel-Kings could be supplemented—reflected in the Greek title of the book *ta paralipomena*, 'the things left out'. In Noth's work the Chronicler becomes an author who selected his material to tell a different story about Israel from the one told by the Deuteronomistic Historian—a much more upbeat story. In the process he was content simply to copy out much of the deuteronomistic material, but in what he added and (just as important) in what he left out, he showed us his own *Tendenz*. For example, his picture of David as a national hero is achieved by omitting the darker side of David that emerges in 2 Samuel, with the story of David's adultery with Bathsheba and murder of her husband Uriah simply left out. The Chronicler's David is not the same as the Deuteronomist's David: and consequently neither is 'the real David'.

COMPOSITION CRITICISM

Redaction criticism has waned somewhat in the English-speaking world of late, being replaced by some of the movements to be considered next. But in German scholarship it is still relatively dominant, sometimes in the form of 'composition criticism', where one analyses the various stages by which a biblical book has been put together and asks about what motives lie behind each stage. This is obviously possible in principle, but it strikes many English-speaking critics as over-optimistic about the practicalities, and indeed all varieties of redaction criticism invite this kind of scepticism: can we really be sure that a small verbal change in one particular verse is a deliberate attempt to give the surrounding passage a new orientation? Redaction criticism assumes that changes in copying manuscripts are always deliberate and full of intention, and tends to disregard the possibility that sometimes scribes were careless and added material loosely from memory, or (conversely) copied out passages that were not entirely to their own taste just because they were there in the document in front of them. The possibility of accident and casualness in the production of the Bible is seriously underestimated in much redaction criticism. That said, it is perhaps even less in evidence in the approaches to be surveyed next.

STRUCTURALISM

Redaction criticism may be seen, and certainly saw itself, as regaining a sense of the biblical text as literature, with authors or at any rate compilers who were trying to convey something by the way they edited older material. They were not authors in quite the modern sense, since they were not creating literature from nothing, but their shaping and refashioning of older sources was a creative, author-like activity. Not long after redaction criticism got under way, however, other developments were taking place in the wider world of literary studies that called in question the importance of authors anyway, and shifted critical attention on to 'the text itself', as an independently existing phenomenon whose meaning was not determined by its author, but by the possibilities of the literary system in which it belonged. This movement, which started in

France but was taken up with enthusiasm by many scholars in the English-speaking world (less so in Germany), was known as structuralism.

SOCIAL ANTHROPOLOGY AND LINGUISTICS

Structuralism did not originally develop within literary studies but in two other fields: social anthropology and linguistics. Both fields had by the 1970s developed theories according to which meaning derives from the structures of institutions, rather than from the intentions of specific people. For example, social anthropologists study kinship structures—the interrelationship between the members of families. There are societies like most in Western Europe, where it is normal to marry outside the family, and others, common in other parts of the world, where marriages between cousins or even half-siblings are usual, and where it is shameful to marry a complete outsider. Again, there are societies where the most important male family-member is one's father, but others where it is one's uncle. Now which kind of society one lives in determines the meaning of one's action in getting married. If I belong to the endogamous (marrying in) kind of society and I instead marry out, then, *irrespective of whether or not I intend it*, I send out a particular message, one that may be serious enough to get me killed or ostracized. Similarly, when we speak a language we do not determine the meaning of the words we use: the meaning is a given, and people will understand my words according to public conventions—the language is not mine to reshape or redefine. If I *say*, 'I like tomatoes', it is no use claiming that I really *meant* 'you detest bananas'. My freedom of speech is not freedom to make words mean anything I like, as Humpty-Dumpty famously claimed in *Alice in Wonderland*. A language forms a system, and speakers are constrained by that system.

LITERARY STRUCTURALISM

Literary structuralists claimed that literature is a system just like kinship or language, in which meaning is generated not by the intentions of authors but by the structures of the literary conventions in force at the time. We can see this clearly if we think about literary genre. A novel is not the same as a play, which is not the same as a lyric poem. Each of these three genres sets up certain expectations in the reader. Applying the point to the Bible, a Gospel is not the same kind of thing as an Epistle, and we should feel that something was wrong if in the middle of a Gospel we suddenly found a piece of correspondence, or if in the middle of an Epistle we found a section of narrative—indeed, we should probably go into source-critical mode and suggest that the books in question were composite. A Gospel necessarily tells a story, just as an Epistle necessarily conveys ideas the writer wants the reader to accept. The structuralist message is that the kind of content each genre has is predetermined, and has little or nothing to do with the intentions of the writer. The text is in a sense authorless: it is a product of the system of literature.

Almost everyone will find this claim exaggerated. We may be constrained so far as the *kind* of information we can convey in a given genre is concerned, but surely within those constraints it is possible to produce original work. A lyric poem is not the right genre to convey information about how to use a washing-machine (though a good comic poem could be produced that did this), but there is still a vast range of thoughts that it can be used to convey, and these are not determined by the genre. Nevertheless, the basic structuralist idea that literature is a system is a fruitful one, and it reminds us how far our thoughts and expressions are given in the system, and are often less original than we might like to think. As applied to the Bible, structuralism stressed the way in which ideas are conveyed through the shape of the text, and this is an important addition to the usual kinds of interpretation. For example, the opening passage of Genesis overtly tells us things abut the creation of the world. But beneath the surface it tells us other things by the way it is structured. It breaks into two equal halves, ending with the third day and the sixth day respectively, each half having almost exactly the same number of words, and with a pattern in each half according to which there is one act of creation on days 1 and 2 and on days 4 and 5, but two acts on days 3 and 6. This conveys a sense of order in the world over and above anything the writer actually says. Indeed, it conveys this sense even if we speculate that it may be an accident, unintended by the writer—the text just happened to turn out that way. Its meaning is not dependent on the author's intention, but simply on observable structures in the text.

Structuralists believed that writing is always more or less according to a formula. That is more obvious in some genres—detective novels, say, or sonnets—than it is in others. But ultimately all texts have patterns, and those patterns are generated by literary conventions, not by the originality of authors. To many readers, who think that the best literature is precisely the literature that is most original, this seemed counter-intuitive; but it certainly does have its uses in helping to explain why we react to literature as we do. And arguably the Bible is a particularly fertile field for structuralist analysis, since so much of its material is clearly very conventional. In reading a book such as Proverbs, for example, it helps to know that we are not encountering the highly original thoughts of King Solomon, but the traditional wisdom of centuries, expressed in highly stylized forms. The meaning of Proverbs, or of any given proverb within the book, does not depend on the thinking of an original 'author', but is generated by the structures of Israelite tradition. Much the same may be true of the Psalms which, as we have seen, are not an individual's lyric poems, but reusable expressions of the religious sentiments of a people.

NEW CRITICISM

Somewhat earlier than the beginnings of structuralism in France, American literary criticism had produced a movement nowadays usually called the 'New Criticism', which starting from a quite different intellectual position had reached not dissimilar conclusions about the unimportance of authors. This movement never affected biblical studies directly, though there are strong resemblances to it in 'canonical criticism' (discussed later). For the New Critics texts were free-standing entities, which did not need to be interpreted against a historical background, still less with any concern about their authors' intentions. In principle one could read a text as if in a vacuum, asking questions entirely about the meaning generated by this particular assemblage of words on paper and ignoring all context. This is in its way not unlike structuralism, in that the object of interpretation is quite strictly the text itself, and not the intentions of its author: New Critics produced the term 'The Intentional

Fallacy'. In New Criticism as in structuralism there is an exclusive concentration on texts themselves which destroys all interest in the skill of the author: texts are seen almost as self-generated.

Structuralism and New Criticism set the agenda for literary study in the 1960s and 1970s, so that many biblical critics (outside the German-speaking world) started to think that the traditional concern with the biblical writers, which we find reaching its highpoint in redaction criticism, had been misguided. More and more scholars produced analyses of biblical passages that sought to uncover their underlying structure and shape and that ignored questions of date, setting, and authorship.

POSTSTRUCTURALISM

The present period of biblical studies has seen plenty of traditional approaches to the Bible continuing in strength. Many scholars continue to practise redaction criticism; books are still written on the sources of the Gospels or the Pentateuch; the historical background of the biblical texts continues to be a major focus, as we have seen; and there is still a lot of work done, and to be done, on establishing accurate texts of both Old and New Testaments. In a humanities subject such as biblical studies new movements do not simply sweep away all that came before, as they tend to do in the sciences. But there are trends, and one of these continues the tendency to follow the wider literary world and thus engage with the major movement that followed structuralism, which goes variously by the name of poststructuralism or (a somewhat broader term) postmodernism. This represents a next logical move after structuralism.

THE READER

For structuralists, as for New Critics, what matters is *the text itself*, shorn of any context. But in certain postmodernist circles, following the lead of Jacques Derrida, the text itself has disappeared much as the author did in structuralism. For the text is seen as part of a continuum which includes also the reader. The text is not something objective, 'out there', but exists only when it is activated by a reader, rather as a piece of music can be said to exist only when it is being performed. This is made overt in certain forms of 'reader-response criticism', in which meaning does not inhere in the text but is contributed to the text by the reader. A famous saying sums this up by saying that a text is like a picnic, to which the author brings the words and the reader brings the meaning. Once we abandon the author as the source of meaning, this may be a logical outcome: the structuralist or New Critical idea that one can find a point of repose in the text itself is now seen to be more conservative than it appears, and as really only a staging-post on the way to a postmodernist conviction that text and reader interact to produce a meaning (not *the* meaning—for what the meaning is depends on who is doing the reading).

'READINGS'

These postmodern ideas are proving influential in biblical studies, even as more traditional styles of biblical criticism continue to be practised. They are obviously vulnerable to the criticism that once one travels down this road, anything goes: all objectivity has been abandoned, and there is a free-for-all. In place of an exegesis of the text—that is, an attempt to say what it 'really means'—we have only *readings*, which may be more or less appealing, more or less good for us, more or less influential, but not more or less true. 'Readings', indeed, is the title of an important series of commentaries on individual biblical books. I can compare two people's readings of a text and decide that I prefer one to the other, but I cannot adjudicate between them on any objective basis, for the reading I produce through this adjudication will still be only a reading—my reading. Along this line of thought there is now a very great interest in the history of the reception of the Bible, looking at what in various generations (and in various media: artistic, musical, literary) it has been taken to mean. Sometimes this interest is itself a historical interest, which produces extremely fascinating insights, and it was mentioned in chapter 1. The history of biblical interpretation, after all, should not be simply the history of technical, 'professional' biblical scholarship but should take in other media, and should also include a study of how the Bible has been read at a popular level. But sometimes reception history has a clearly postmodern agenda, saying in effect that a text can mean anything it has been taken to mean. In studying reception history one needs to be clear whether or not one accepts this tenet. Some reception historians do, some don't.

NEWER LITERARY APPROACHES

At the same time as all these theoretical developments were taking place, some critics coming from the literary world rather than from the world of biblical studies began to take an interest in the Bible in a non-theoretical way and to read it as they would read any other literary work. Such critics knew about New Criticism, of course, and also about structuralism and poststructuralism, but they were concerned to read the biblical books without applying masses of theory, to undertake what in literary circles is known as a 'close reading' of the text. This was not usually greatly concerned with the intentions of the authors (and it was often pointed out that anyway many of the biblical books are anonymous and the product of more than one period of time), but nor did it require an insistent looking away from authorial intention. Often in reading the Bible in this literary way literary critics became sceptical about source-critical theories, arguing that the texts really hang together much more tightly than the source critics had thought; but, again, there is no hostility to the possibility of sources in principle. Outstanding examples of literary scholars who have read the Bible in this way are Frank Kermode, Gabriel Josipovici, and Robert Alter. They all tend to read for unity in texts that many have deemed composite, and they make the point that even if the text was composite in its origins, it does now exist in a finished form and should be read as it stands, not simply 'excavated' like an archaeological site.

CANONICAL CRITICISM

Attention to the text just as it stands, rather than to hypothetical stages that lie behind it, is a strong feature of the newer literary approaches. But it can also be found in a distinctively theological approach that is generally described as 'canonical criticism', though its founder, Brevard Childs (1923–2007), consistently avoided this term and called it simply 'the canonical approach'. The interest in the Bible as a canon (or, as it is sometimes put, as Scripture) arises not from applying secular literary standards to the text, but from the conviction that the Bible is a special case for Jewish and Christian believers, and needs to be treated with what might be called a 'special hermeneutic', that is, with tools and methods appropriate to its scriptural status. The theological inspiration behind this idea comes from the great Swiss theologian Karl Barth (1886–1968), but it is not original to him: it underlay much Bible-reading in the ancient Church and can be found also in the Protestant Reformers of the sixteenth century. In many ways it is similar to the 'non-critical' way of reading the Bible outlined in chapter 1. It involves reading books of the Bible as true, relevant, profound, and self-consistent, and also as according with the Church's confession of faith. Though the canonical approach is new within modern biblical studies, it is thus in many ways a return to 'pre-critical' modes of reading Scripture, and it has been both applauded and criticized for this.

HOLISTIC READING

In many ways—but not all. For one of the major concerns of the canonical approach is to read biblical books as complete wholes, concentrating on their 'final form' rather than on underlying strata; and in this respect it has more in common with the newer literary approaches just discussed, and even with structuralism and New Criticism. Childs always denied that he had been influenced by any literary models, but there is no reason why we should not notice the similarities, even if we cannot speak of influence. The interest in the final form of books did not much characterize pre-critical reading, and in this Childs's approach is distinctly modern and 'postcritical'. In the early Church as in rabbinic Judaism books were commonly thought of as wholes—thus the book of Isaiah was treated as coming entirely from the prophet of that name, not dissected into First, Second, and Third Isaiah, together with a mass of fragments coming from none of them—but there was seldom an attempt to read the books as unified 'works' in the way we now read a novel. They tended to be treated as collections of individual sayings, each capable of being interpreted on its own, as in the idea of the 'text' for a sermon, which is usually a small portion, maybe even a single verse, from a larger book.

Now this method is eschewed in the canonical approach, which concentrates on finding unity even in books, like Isaiah, that really do appear to many critics to be collections of fragments. And this is new. If applied, say, to the Gospels (on the whole it has been more used in Old Testament studies) it would take us well beyond redaction criticism, into a world where the Gospel precisely in its present form expresses the faith of the Church as a whole, not the thinking of its compiler. Canonical criticism is a highly 'confessional' form of reading the Bible, which takes the finished form of the Bible as its starting-point, on the basis that it is this form of the text that the Church has handed down to us.

PROBLEMS IN CANONICAL CRITICISM

There are many possible criticisms of the canonical approach. For example, we have to ask what is meant by the 'final form' of the text. Is it the Hebrew text we find in most Hebrew Bibles, which is a copy of a manuscript dating from the eleventh century AD (the Leningrad Codex), and in most Greek New Testaments, which is an 'eclectic' text, the best guesses of modern editors about what the Greek New Testament originally said? Or is it some putative text underlying all these, in which case it is actually unavailable to us? Does the fact that a book exists as a unit mean that it has to be interpreted as a unity? Do we know in advance that any given book will turn out to have a 'message' fully compatible with the Church's teaching? After all, the Reformation often argued that the Bible did not mean what the Church had traditionally taken it to mean. And did the Church, in giving us these books, also give us an interpretative method to go with them? All these are difficult questions, and it has yet to be seen whether canonical critics can give them a convincing answer. Yet the approach has been influential, and not only on those who accept it fully. Perhaps more importantly, it has moved the discussion of biblical interpretation on by insisting that, alongside literary questions, the reader of the Bible should also ask about its religious message, and should take an interest (to put it no higher) in the meaning of whole books, not simply of fragments or sources. After all, Genesis exists now in a way that J and P do not: it is there when we open a Bible. It is far from foolish to suggest that we should ask what Genesis means. Answering that question, however, is far from simple.

ADVOCACY READINGS

Alongside these more literary and theological movements in the study of the Bible the twentieth century saw the rise of approaches to the biblical text based more in various social concerns. Marx said that the point was not merely to understand the world but to change it, and some biblical interpreters argued in a similar vein that what mattered was not to understand the Bible ('objectively', as critics have sometimes put it), but to read it in such a way that it becomes world-changing.

LIBERATION THEOLOGY

The first such movement to emerge was a style of biblical inter-pretation bound up with liberation theology. Liberation theologians argued not only that God's 'preferential option for the poor' was something the modern Church should recognize and act on, help-ing to end the oppression of millions in the Third World (but not only there), but also that this was the message of the Bible, which generations of politically conservative critics had ignored or inter-preted away. Any worthwhile biblical interpretation should read the Bible with an eye to this divine imperative; any reading that ignored it amounted to connivance with the powerful against the interests of the poor.

Now liberationist readings are not simply one more possible mode of criticism to set alongside the others we have been exam-ining. They require a revisionist understanding of all approaches to the Bible. This can be seen in the massive influence of Norman K. Gottwald's *The Tribes of Yahweh*, published in 1979. This took a clearly liberationist perspective. But in the process it actually rewrote the early history of Israel as that had hitherto been under-stood, arguing (as we saw in chapter 5) for the origins of Israel in a kind of peasants' revolt within the Canaanite city-state structures. This radically reinterpreted the story told in Joshua and Judges. Gottwald did not argue that his theory was true in spite of these biblical books, but that properly read they supported his theory.

Thus a liberationist reading actually had consequences for exegesis at a fairly basic level. Liberation theology was not an (optional) extra layer in interpretation, but the prerequisite for understanding properly what the Bible was saying.

Two themes emerged particularly strongly in liberationist readings: the centrality of the exodus—the rescue of Israel, the underdogs, from slavery in Egypt; and the teaching of the prophets on social justice. These themes constituted the centre of the Old Testament, just as the idea of liberation from oppression dominated the teaching of Jesus in the New Testament. Such ideas provided a hermeneutical key to reading the Bible: any reading that did not pay attention to them was necessarily flawed, and derived from collaboration with oppression. Biblical interpretation properly understood is not a game played by scholars, but a matter of life and death for millions of oppressed people around the world. Traditional biblical criticism, it is argued, tends to ignore this moral demand and to take refuge in a quest for 'objective' meanings that are actually the meanings preferred by the oppressors.

Thus liberation theology questions the validity of the entire enterprise of biblical criticism as that has come down to us, and seeks to put something new in its place, something that will make the Bible fruitful in changing the world. At times this may entail challenges to the apparent meaning of the biblical text, since (for example) both Testaments seem to envisage the institution of slavery as tolerable or even right. In such cases the hermeneutical key comes into operation, and downgrades such passages by comparison with those that teach liberation—very much as traditional Lutheran readings of the New Testament downplay passages that seem to speak of justification by works, on the grounds that justification by faith is far more centrally the message of the New Testament.

FEMINIST CRITICISM

A subset of liberation theology, in many ways, is feminist biblical criticism. Here the oppressed are identified as women, but the approach to interpreting the texts is somewhat more nuanced than in liberation theology in general. There is disagreement among feminist scholars about how objectionable the biblical text is: some argue that it is irredeemably patriarchal, others that it is much less patriarchal than one would expect, given the kind of culture it comes from. Feminists of the second kind tend to study the portrayal of women in the biblical text and to draw attention to positive images of women, arguing that these should steer our reading of the Bible in general—much as the option for the poor should guide interpretation, according to liberation theology.

Among those who see the Bible as oppressive to women, two strategies are open. The first is to reject the Bible and thus to move away from biblical interpretation altogether into what are seen as more fruitful kinds of theology. But the second is to adopt what is often called a 'resistant reading', in which the biblical record is reconfigured as it might have been if written from a more feminist standpoint. Thus, notoriously, the prophet Ezekiel seems to regard sexual violence towards women as an acceptable metaphor for God's punishment of his people (Ezekiel 16 and 23). Resistant readers will take this abhorrent argument and use it to challenge modern readers to reconsider their own attitudes to women and to relations between the sexes in general, reading Ezekiel, as it is sometimes put, 'against the grain'.

OBJECTIVE AND SUBJECTIVE

One difficulty with feminist, and other liberationist, styles of interpretation is to know where they stand on the question of whether biblical interpretation should be 'objective' or 'subjective'. On the whole writers from both these movements regard the word 'objective' as one applied in bad faith by oppressive/male critics to justify their own oppressive readings and make them appear the only feasible readings. But in another sense liberationist and feminist readers are themselves seeking to identify an objective meaning in the text—to argue that the Bible, *properly read*, supports liberation for the poor and for women. The word 'properly' is crucial here. Neither group wishes to suggest that we can adopt liberationist/ feminist readings if we so choose, but that we *ought* to do so. And this must mean that the text forces such an option upon us; in other words, that such is the objective meaning of the text. It is a high claim and an important one, and there is risk in diluting it by treating the word 'objective' as the exclusive possession of the enemy.

Liberationist and feminist criticism are not really a type of reader-response criticism, arguing that 'we choose to read the text in this way', but claim higher ground than that. That makes them vulnerable to opponents who might argue that the Bible says less about the preferential option for the poor than one might wish; or that the exodus is not about the liberation of slaves but about the triumph of a nation, Israel; or that the Bible really does encourage the subordination of women. But theories that are not vulnerable to criticism are not very interesting, and it is probably worth conceding the possibility of being refuted for the sake of making the important claims that liberationist and feminist critics do make.

THE FUTURE OF BIBLICAL INTERPRETATION

It seems clear that biblical interpretation will continue to include a wide variety of approaches. Claims to have produced *the* definitive way of reading the Bible always fail; in that respect biblical interpretation is part of the humanities, in which there is always a plurality of methods and approaches. One question that has emerged from this survey, and that seems destined to continue to be controversial, is the following: how far are interpretations about the text, and how far are they about the reader? At first sight the answer seems obvious: of course they are about the text. But many of the more recent approaches outlined above claim either that we cannot really know about the text as it is in itself at all, or else that the two questions in the end come down to the same thing, because all knowledge of texts is simultaneously knowledge of ourselves, the readers. In discussing liberationist and feminist interpretation above I suggested that these approaches are more 'objective' in their interests than their own proponents are sometimes willing to allow; but many interpreters in the last half-century would say that the distinction between objective and subjective interpretation is simply meaningless anyway. Reader-response criticism, they would say, is not just one option in biblical interpretation: *all* biblical interpretation is always and necessarily reader-response criticism. It's simply that those who embrace the title of reader-response critic are open and upfront about this, whereas traditional interpreters deceive themselves that they are practising an 'objective' approach.

This issue is sure to rumble on in the present century. It is an issue in aesthetic theory in general, and not peculiar to the study of the Bible: consequently one that biblical scholars are unlikely to resolve on their own. But it may be that biblical scholars have some particularly useful insights to contribute to it, precisely because they spend so much time on the interpretation of a small body of texts that have such a large freight of importance and centrality for millions of people.

FURTHER READING

A general guide to approaches to Old Testament interpretation is provided by John Barton, *Reading the Old Testament: Method in Biblical Study*, second edition, London: Darton, Longman & Todd, 1995; cf. John M. Court, *Reading the New Testament*, London: Routledge, 1997. For a survey of modern and postmodern readings see Yvonne Sherwood (ed.), *Derrida's Bible: Reading a Page of Scripture with a Little Help from Derrida*, New York and Basingstoke: Palgrave Macmillan, 2004. For an overview of biblical interpretation see John Barton (ed.), *The Cambridge Companion to Biblical Interpretation*, Cambridge: Cambridge University Press, 1998.

Literary approaches can be sampled in Frank Kermode and Robert Alter (eds), *The Literary Guide to the Bible*, London: Fontana, 1997, and in works of the two editors: F. Kermode, *The Genesis of Secrecy: On the Interpretation of Narrative*, Cambridge, Mass. and London: Harvard University Press, 1979, and R. Alter, *The Art of Biblical Narrative*, New York: Basic Books, 1981.

For feminist reading there is much in J'annine Jobling, *Feminist Biblical Interpretation in Theological Context: Restless Readings*, Aldershot: Ashgate, 2002, and in the works of Elizabeth Schüssler Fiorenza, for example *Sharing Her Word: Feminist Biblical Interpretation in Context*, Edinburgh: T & T Clark, 1998, and her now classic work *In Memory of Her: A Feminist Theological Reconstruction of Christian Origins*, London: SCM, 1995.

For liberation-theological biblical interpretation see L. and C. Boff, *Introducing Liberation Theology*, Tunbridge Wells: Burns & Oates, 1987, and Norbert Lohfink, *Option for the Poor: The Basic Principle of Liberation Theology in the Light of the Bible*, Berkeley: BIBAL Press, 1987. For an overview of liberation theology as a whole, see Christopher Rowland (ed.), *The Cambridge Companion to Liberation Theology*, Cambridge: Cambridge University Press, 1999.

BIBLIOGRAPHY

Ackroyd, P. R. and C. F. Evans, *The Cambridge History of the Bible*, vol.1, Cambridge: Cambridge University Press, 1963.

Alter, Robert, *The Art of Biblical Narrative*, New York: Basic Books, 1981.

Ashton, John, *The Interpretation of John*, Edinburgh: T & T Clark, 1997.

Aune, D. E., *The New Testament in its Literary Environment*, Philadelphia: Westminster, 1987.

Barr, James, *The Bible in the Modern World*, London: SCM, 1973.

Barton, John (ed.), *The Cambridge Companion to Biblical Interpretation*, Cambridge: Cambridge University Press, 1998.

Barton, John, *What is the Bible?* London: SPCK, 2009 (third edition).

——, *The Nature of Biblical Criticism*, Louisville, Ky. and London: Westminster John Knox, 2007.

——, *Ethics and the Old Testament*, London: SCM Press, second edition 2002.

——, *The Spirit and the Letter: Studies in the Biblical Canon*, London: SPCK, 1998 (American edition *Holy Writings, Sacred Text: The Canon in Early Christianity*, Louisville, Ky.: Westminster John Knox, 1998).

——, *Making the Christian Bible*, London: Darton, Longman & Todd, 1997 (American edition *How the Bible Came to Be*, Louisville, Ky.: Westminster John Knox, 1997).

——, *Reading the Old Testament: Method in Biblical Study*, London: Darton, Longman & Todd, 1995 (second edition).

——, *Oracles of God: Perceptions of Ancient Prophecy in Israel after the Exile*, London: Darton, Longman & Todd, 2007 (second edition).

Bauckham, Richard, *The Gospels for All Christians: Rethinking the Gospel Audiences*, Edinburgh: T & T Clark, 1998.

Beckwith, Roger, *The Old Testament Canon of the New Testament Church and its Background in Early Judaism*, Grand Rapids, Mich.: Eerdmans, 1986.

Blenkinsopp, Joseph, *A History of Prophecy in Israel*, Louisville, Ky.: Westminster John Knox, second edition 1996.

——, *Wisdom and Law in the Old Testament: The Ordering of Law in Israel and Early Judaism*, Oxford: Oxford University Press, 1995.

Bockmuehl, Markus, *Seeing the Word: Refocusing New Testament Study*, Grand Rapids, Mich.: Baker Academic, 2006.

Boff, L. and C., *Introducing Liberation Theology*, Tunbridge Wells: Burns & Oates, 1987.

Borg, M., *Jesus in Contemporary Scholarship*, Valley Forge, Pa.: Trinity Press International, 1994.

Bornkamm, Günther, *Jesus of Nazareth*, London: Hodder & Stoughton, 1963.

Brooke, George, 'The Dead Sea Scrolls', in John Barton (ed.), *The Biblical World*, London: Routledge, 2002.

Brueggemann, Walter, *Theology of the Old Testament: Testimony, Dispute, Advocacy*, Minneapolis: Fortress, 1997.

Burridge, Richard, *What are the Gospels? A Comparison with Graeco-Roman Biography*, Cambridge: Cambridge University Press, 1992.

Collins, John J., *The Apocalyptic Imagination: An Introduction to Jewish Apocalyptic Literature*, Grand Rapids, Mich.: Eerdmans, 1998 (second edition).

Conzelmann, Hans, *The Theology of St Luke*, London: Faber & Faber, 1969.

Court, John M., *Reading the New Testament*, London: Routledge, 1997.

Crenshaw, James L., *Old Testament Wisdom: An Introduction*, Louisville, Ky.: Westminster John Knox, 1998 (second edition).

——, *Theodicy in the Old Testament*, London: SPCK, 1983.

Crossan, J. D., *The Birth of Christianity*, Edinburgh: T & T Clark, 1999.

Dawkins, Richard, *River out of Eden: A Darwinian View of Life*, London: Phoenix, 1995.

Day, John, *The Psalms*, Sheffield: Sheffield Academic Press, 1992.

Dell, Katharine J., *Get Wisdom, Get Insight: An Introduction to Israel's Wisdom Literature*, London: Darton, Longman & Todd, 2000.

Dunn, J. D. G., *The New Perspective on Paul: Collected Essays*, Tübingen: Mohr Siebeck, 2005.

——, *Christology in the Making: A New Testament Inquiry into the Origins of the Doctrine of the Incarnation*, London: SCM, 1989 (second edition).

Esler, Philip, *The First Christians in their Social World: Social-Scientific Approaches to New Testament Interpretation*, London: Routledge, 1994.

Frye, C. Northrop, *The Great Code: The Bible and Literature*, London: Routledge & Kegan Paul, 1982.

Gamble, Harry Y., 'Letters in the New Testament and in the Graeco-Roman World', in John Barton (ed.), *The Biblical World*, vol. 1, London: Routledge, 2002.

Gillingham, Susan, *The Poems and Psalms of the Hebrew Bible*, Oxford: Oxford University Press, 1994.

Goodman, Martin, *Rome and Jerusalem: The Clash of Ancient Civilizations*, London: Allen Lane, 2007.

Gottwald, Norman K., *The Tribes of Yahweh*, London: SCM Press, 1979.

Grabbe, L. L., *Ancient Israel: What do we Know and How do we Know it?* London: T & T Clark, 2007.

——, *A History of Jews and Judaism in the Second Temple Period*, London: T & T Clark, 2004.

——, *An Introduction to First Century Judaism: Jewish Religion and History in the Second Temple Period*, London: T & T Clark, 2004.

——, *Priests, Prophets, Diviners, Sages: A Socio-Historical Study of Religious Specialists in Ancient Israel*, Valley Forge, Pa.: Trinity Press International, 1995.

Greenspoon, Leonard, 'Jewish Bible Translation', in John Barton (ed.), *The Biblical World*, vol. 2, London and New York: Routledge, 2002.

Gunn, David M. and Danna Nolan Fewell, *Narrative in the Hebrew Bible*, Oxford: Oxford University Press, 1993.

Hayes J. H. and J. M. Miller, *Israelite and Judaean History*, Philadelphia: Trinity Press International, 1977.

Hays, Richard B., *The Moral Vision of the New Testament*, Edinburgh: T & T Clark, 1997.

Hengel, Martin, *The Four Gospels and the One Gospel of Jesus Christ*, London: SCM, 2000.

Hurtado, Larry, *One God, One Lord: Early Christian Devotion and Ancient Jewish Monotheism*, Edinburgh: T & T Clark, 1998 (second edition).

Jobling, J'annine, *Feminist Biblical Interpretation in Theological Context: Restless Readings*, Aldershot: Ashgate, 2002.

Kermode, Frank, *The Genesis of Secrecy: On the Interpretation of Narrative*, Cambridge, Mass. and London: Harvard University Press, 1979.

Kermode, Frank and Robert Alter (eds), *The Literary Guide to the Bible*, London: Fontana, 1997.

Kratz, R. G., *The Composition of the Narrative Books of the Old Testament*, London: T & T Clark, 2005.

Lim, Timothy, *The Dead Sea Scrolls: A Very Short Introduction*, Oxford: Oxford University Press, 2005.

Lohfink, Norbert, *Option for the Poor: The Basic Principle of Liberation Theology in the Light of the Bible*, Berkeley: BIBAL Press, 1987.

Metzger, Bruce M., *The Bible in Translation: Ancient and English Versions*, Grand Rapids, Mich.: Baker Academic, 2001.

——, *The New Testament Canon: Its Origin, Development, and Significance*, Oxford: Clarendon Press, 1987.

Miller, J. M., *The Old Testament and the Historian*, London: SPCK, 1976.

Moberly, R. W. L., *The Bible, Theology, and Faith: A Study of Abraham and Jesus*, Cambridge: Cambridge University Press, 2000.

Morgan, Robert, 'Jesus', in John Barton (ed.), *The Biblical World*, London: Routledge, 2002.

Muddiman, John, *The Bible: Fountain and Well of Truth*, Oxford: Basil Blackwell, 1983.

Noth, Martin, *The Deuteronomistic History*, Sheffield: JSOT Press, 1981 (from the German original of 1943).

Pearce, Sarah, 'Judaea under Roman Rule, 63 BCE–135CE', in John Barton (ed.), *The Biblical World*, London: Routledge, 2002.

Porter, J. R., *The Lost Bible: Forgotten Scriptures Revealed*, London: Duncan Baird Publishers, 2001.

Räisänen, Heikki, *Paul and the Law*, Tübingen: Mohr, 1983.

Robinson, J. M., *A New Quest of the Historical Jesus*, London: SCM Press, 1959.

Rowland, Christopher (ed.), *The Cambridge Companion to Liberation Theology*, Cambridge: Cambridge University Press, 1999.

Sanders, E. P., *The Historical Figure of Jesus*, London: Allen Lane—the Penguin Press, 1993.

——, *Jesus and Judaism*, London: SCM, 1985.

——, *Paul, the Law, and the Jewish People*, Philadelphia: Fortress Press, 1985.

Sanders, E. P. and Margaret Davies, *Studying the Synoptic Gospels*, London: SCM, 1989.

Schüssler Fiorenza, Elizabeth, *Sharing Her Word: Feminist Biblical Interpretation in Context*, Edinburgh: T & T Clark, 1998,

——, *In Memory of Her: A Feminist Theological Reconstruction of Christian Origins*, London: SCM, 1995.

Sherwood, Yvonne (ed.), *Derrida's Bible: Reading a Page of Scripture with a Little Help from Derrida*, New York and Basingstoke: Palgrave Macmillan, 2004.

Theissen, Gerd and Dagmar Winter, *The Quest for the Plausible Jesus*, London: SCM Press, 2002.

Theissen, Gerd, *The Shadow of the Galilean: The Quest of the Historical Jesus in Narrative Form*, London: SCM Press, 1982.

Vaux, R. de, *Ancient Israel: Its Life and Institutions*, London: Darton, Longman & Todd, 1973.

Vermes, Geza, *Jesus the Jew: A Historian's Reading of the Gospels*, London: SCM Press, 2001 (sixth edition).

Wansbrough, Henry, 'Christian Bible Translation', in John Barton (ed.), *The Biblical World*, vol. 2, London and New York: Routledge, 2002.

Watson, Francis, *Text, Church and World: Biblical Interpretation in Theological Perspective*, Edinburgh: T & T Clark, 1994.

Wellhausen, Julius, *Prolegomena to the History of Israel*, 1878 (reprinted as *Prolegomena to the History of Ancient Israel*, New York, 1957).

Williams, Catrin H., 'Interpretation of the Identity and Role of Jesus', in John Barton (ed.), *The Biblical World*, vol. 2, London: Routledge, 2002.

Williamson, H. G. M. (ed.), *Understanding the History of Ancient Israel*, Oxford: Oxford University Press for the British Academy, 2007.

Wills, Lawrence M., *The Jewish Novel in the Ancient World*, Ithaca & London: Cornell University Press, 1995.

Wright, C. J. H., *Old Testament Ethics for the People of God*, Leicester: Intervarsity Press, 2004.

Wright, N. T., *Jesus and the Victory of God*, London: SPCK, 1996.

——, *The Climax of the Covenant: Christ and the Law in Pauline Theology*, Edinburgh: T & T Clark, 1991.

INDEX